Red Hot Chili Peppers

Cover photo by David Atlas/Retna Ltd.

ISBN 0-634-09648-6

HAL•LEONARD®
CORPORATION
7777 W. BLUEMOUND RD. P.O. BOX 13819 MILWAUKEE, WI 53213

For all works contained herein:
Unauthorized copying, arranging, adapting, recording or public performance is an infringement of copyright.

Contents

Aeroplane

Words and Music by Anthony Kiedis,
Flea, Chad Smith and David Navarro

I like pleas-ure spiked _ with pain and

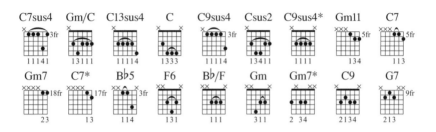

Intro

| C7sus4 | Gm/C | C13sus4 | C | |
| C9sus4 | Csus2 | C9sus4* | C | |

Chorus 1

Gm11   C7
I like pleasure spiked with pain and music is my aeroplane,

Gm11   C7
It's my areo-plane.

Gm11   C7
Songbird sweet and sour Jane, and music is my aeroplane,

Gm11   C7
It's my aero-plane.

                    Gm11
Pleasure spiked with pain,

C7   Gm11   C7
   That motherfucker's always   spiked with pain.

© 1995 THREE POUNDS OF LOVE MUSIC
All Rights Reserved   Used by Permission

Verse 1

    Gm7   C7*
A looking in my own eyes, ___ hello,

Gm7   C7*
I can find the love I want.

Gm7   C7*
Someone better slap me   before I start to

Gm7   C7*
Rust, before I start to decompose.

Gm7   C7*
Looking in my rear view mir-ror.

Gm7   C7*
Looking in my rear view mir-ror,

Gm7   C7*
I can make it disappear.

Gm7   C7*
  I can make it disap-pear, have no fear.

Chorus 2   *Repeat Chorus 1*

Verse 2

Gm7   C7*
Sitting in my kitchen,   hey, girl,

  Gm7   C7*
I'm turning into dust again.

  Gm7   C7*
My melancholy baby,   the star of mazzy

Gm7   C7*
Must push her voice in-side of me.

  Gm7   C7*
I'm overcoming gravity.

  Gm7   C7*
I'm overcoming gravity.

  Gm7   C7*
It's easy when you're sad to be.

  Gm7   C7*
It's easy when you're sad,   saddle up me.

Chorus 3

Gm11   C7
I like pleasure spiked with pain and music is my aeroplane,

Gm11   C7
It's my aero-plane.

Gm11   C7
Songbird sweet and sour Jane, and music is my aeroplane,

Gm11   C7
It's my aero-plane.

Bridge

                    B♭5   F6
Pleasure spiked ___ with pain.

| B♭/F Gm | B♭5 F6 | B♭/F Gm |

B♭5   F6   B♭/F   Gm
Just one note could make me float, could make ___ me float away.

B♭5   F6   B♭/F   Gm
One note from the song she wrote could fuck me where I lay.

B♭5   F6   B♭/F   Gm
Just one note could make me choke, one note that's not a lie.

B♭5   F6   Gm
Just one note could cut my throat, one note could make me die.

Chorus 4

Gm11   C7
I like pleasure spiked with pain and music is my aeroplane,

Gm11   C7
It's my aero-plane.

Gm11   C7
Songbird sweet and sour Jane, and music is my aeroplane,

Gm11   C7
It's my aero-plane that's spiked with

Bass Solo   ‖: N.C.(Gm7) | (C7)   :‖ *Play 4 times*
                       Pain.

Guitar Solo ‖: Gm7* | C9   :‖ *Play 8 times*
                 | G7 |

Around the World

Words and Music by Anthony Kiedis,
Flea, John Frusciante and Chad Smith

Melody:

All a-round the world   we could make time,

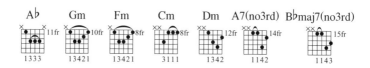

Ab   Gm   Fm   Cm   Dm   A7(no3rd)   Bbmaj7(no3rd)

Intro

‖: N.C.(E5) | :‖

| N.C.(G5) | |

Verse 1

N.C.(G5)

All around the world we could make time,

Rompin' and a stompin' 'cause I'm in my prime.

Born in the north and sworn to entertain ya,

'Cause I'm down for the state of Pennsylvania.

I try not to whine but I must warn ya

'Bout the mother fuckin' girls from California.

Alabama baby said, "Hallelujah,"

Good God, girl, I wish I knew ya.

© 1999 MOEBETOBLAME MUSIC
All Rights Reserved   Used by Permission

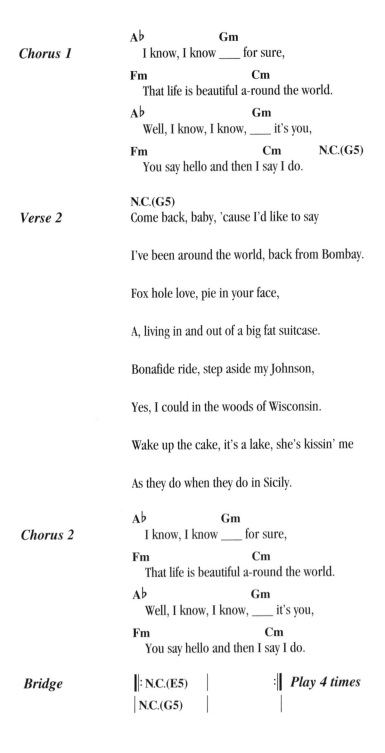

Chorus 1

Ab   Gm
 I know, I know ____ for sure,

Fm   Cm
 That life is beautiful a-round the world.

Ab   Gm
 Well, I know, I know, ____ it's you,

Fm   Cm   N.C.(G5)
 You say hello and then I say I do.

Verse 2

N.C.(G5)
Come back, baby, 'cause I'd like to say

I've been around the world, back from Bombay.

Fox hole love, pie in your face,

A, living in and out of a big fat suitcase.

Bonafide ride, step aside my Johnson,

Yes, I could in the woods of Wisconsin.

Wake up the cake, it's a lake, she's kissin' me

As they do when they do in Sicily.

Chorus 2

Ab   Gm
 I know, I know ____ for sure,

Fm   Cm
 That life is beautiful a-round the world.

Ab   Gm
 Well, I know, I know, ____ it's you,

Fm   Cm
 You say hello and then I say I do.

Bridge

‖: N.C.(E5) | :‖ *Play 4 times*

| N.C.(G5) | |

Verse 3

N.C.(G5)
Where you want to go? Who you want to be?

What you want to do? Just come with me.

I saw God and I saw the fountains,

You and me, girl, sittin' in the Swiss mountains.

Me, oh, my, oh, me and Guy o,

Freer than a bird 'cause we're rockin' Ohio.

Around the world I feel dutiful;

Take a wife 'cause life is beautiful.

Chorus 3

A♭   Gm
I know, I know ___ for sure,

Fm   Cm
$ % % & * * * # # # $ ^ & $ & * #.

A♭   Gm
Well, I know, I know ___ it's you,

Fm   Cm
$ % % & * * * # # # $ ^ & $ & * #.

A♭
Mother Russia, do not suffer,

Gm
I know you're bold enough.

   Fm   Cm
I've been around the world and I have seen your love.

A♭   Gm
I know, I know ___ it's you,

Fm   N.C.(E♭)
You say hello and then I say I do.

Outro

‖: Dm | | A7(no3rd) | B♭maj7(no3rd) :‖ *Play 4 times*

Behind the Sun

Words and Music by Anthony Kiedis, Flea,
Hillel Slovak, Jack Irons and Michael Bienhorn

Melody:

One   day, while bath-ing   in   the   sea, _

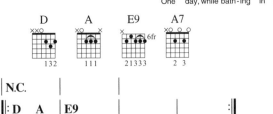

Intro

| N.C. | | |
|:‖: D   A | E9 | | :‖|

Verse 1

E9
One day, while bathing in the sea,

My talkin' dolphin spoke to me.

He spoke to me in symphony,

From freedom's peace beneath the sea.

He looked at me, eyes full of love.

Said, "Yes, we live behind the sun."

Chorus 1

D   A   E9
Behind the sun.

D   A   E9
Behind the sun,

Yeah, yeah, yeah, yeah, yeah, yeah, yeah, yeah,

D   A   E9
Behind the sun.

The sun goes up and the sun goes down,

But like the heart of the sun, my heart continues to pound.

D   A   E9
Behind the sun.

© 1987 MOEBETOBLAME MUSIC, SCREEN GEMS-EMI MUSIC INC. and MORE CUT MUSIC
All Rights Reserved   Used by Permission

                                    E9
Verse 2   Now, while I shower in the rain,

                                    I watch my dolphin swim away.

                                    The one who listens to the surf

                                    Can feel the pulse beat of the earth.

                                    And like my dolphin swims so free,

                                    The sun does swim into the sea.

                                    D   A   E9
Chorus 2   Behind the sun.
                                    D   A   E9
                                    Behind the sun,

                                    Yeah, yeah, yeah, yeah, yeah, yeah, yeah, yeah,
                                    D   A
                                    Behind the sun.
                                    | **E9** | | |
                                    D   A   E9
                                    Behind the sun.

| *Interlude* | ‖: **A7** | | | :‖ |

E9

Verse 3   An island flying through the sky,

One day your son might ask you why.

And if your son should be a girl,

She too might ask you of this world.

The sun shines sweet upon your beach,

And, yes, my dolphin loves to teach.

D   **A**   **E9**

Chorus 3   Behind the sun.

D   **A**   **E9**

Behind the sun,

Yeah, yeah, yeah, yeah, yeah, yeah, yeah, yeah,

D   **A**   **E9**

Behind the sun.

The sun goes up and the sun goes down,

But like the heart of the sun, my heart continues to pound.

D   **A**   **E9**

Behind the sun.   *Wow!*

Blood Sugar Sex Magik

Words and Music by Anthony Kiedis,
Flea, John Frusciante and Chad Smith

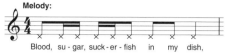

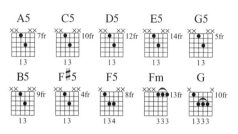

Intro

| A5 | C5 |
|:D5 E5   C5 D5   G5 A5   B5 |
| C5 D5   B5 C5   F#5 G5   A5 C5 :| *Play 3 times*
| D5 E5   C5 D5   G5 A5   B5 |
| C5 D5   B5 C5   F#5 G5 |

Verse 1

N.C.(A5)
Blood, sugar, suckerfish in my dish,

How many pieces do you wish?

Step into a heaven where I keep it on the soul side,

Girl, please me, be my soul bride.

Ev'ry woman has a piece of Aphrodite,

Copulate to create a state of sexual light.

Kissing her virginity, my affinity,

I mingle with the gods, I mingle with divinity.

© 1991 MOEBETOBLAME MUSIC
All Rights Reserved   Used by Permission

Chorus 1

N.C.(E5)
Blood sugar baby, she's magic, sex magic, sex magic.

Blood sugar baby, she's magic, sex magic, sex magic.

Blood sugar crazy, she has it, sex magic, sex magic.

Blood sugar baby, she's magic, sex magic, sex magic.

Bridge

F5	Fm		G		A5 C5
D5 E5	C5 D5	G5 A5	B5	
C5 D5	B5 C5	F#5 G5	A5 C5	
D5 E5	C5 D5	G5 A5	B5	
C5 D5	B5 C5	F#5 G5		

Verse 2

N.C.(A5)
Glorious euphoria is my must,

Erotic shock is a function of lust.

Temporarily blind, dimensions to discover,

In time, each into the other.

Uncontrollable notes from her snow white throat

Fill a space in which two bodies float.

Operatic by voice, a fanatic by choice,

Aromatic is the flower, she must be moist.

Chorus 2	*Repeat Chorus 1*

Interlude 1

N.C.(C5)	(D5)	(C5)	(D5)	
(C5)	(D5)			

Chorus 3	*Repeat Chorus 1*

Interlude 2	*Repeat Interlude 1*

N.C.(E5)

Outro   Blood sugar my girl, she's magic, sex magic, sex magic.

Blood sugar baby, she's magic, sex magic, sex magic.

Blood sugar crazy, she has it, sex magic, sex magic.

Blood sugar baby, she's magic, sex magic, sex magic.

Breaking the Girl

Words and Music by Anthony Kiedis,
Flea, John Frusciante and Chad Smith

Tune down 1/2 step:
(low to high) Eb–Ab–Db–Gb–Bb–Eb

Melody:

I _____ am a man _____

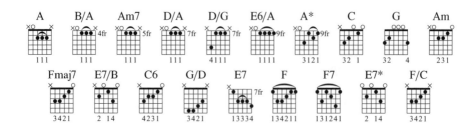

A   B/A   Am7   D/A   D/G   E6/A   A*   C   G   Am

Fmaj7   E7/B   C6   G/D   E7   F   F7   E7*   F/C

Intro

‖: A | B/A Am7 | D/A   D/G D | E6/A   A* :‖

Verse 1

A   B/A   Am7 D/A   D/G   D/A   E6/A   A*
I am a man _____ cut from _____ the know.

A   B/A   Am7 D/A   D/G   D/A   E6/A   A*
Rarely do friends ____ come and _____ then go.

A   B/A   Am7   D/A D/G   D/A   E6/A   A*
She was a girl _____ soft _____ but ___ es-tranged.

A   B/A Am7   D/A D/G   D/A   E6/A   A*
We were the two ___ our lives ____ re - ar-ranged.

Pre-Chorus 1

C   G   Am
Feeling so good that day.

C   G   Fmaj7
A feeling of love that day.

© 1991 MOEBETOBLAME MUSIC
All Rights Reserved   Used by Permission

Chorus 1

```
      Am        E7/B       C6         G/D         E7
```
Twisting and turning, your feelings are burning, you're breaking the girl.

```
Am E7/B C6 G/D F
```
She meant you no   harm.

```
Am          E7/B      C6          G/D         E7
```
Think you're so clever, but now you must sever, you're breaking the girl.

```
Am E7/B C6 G/D F      F7    E7*
```
He   loves no one   else.

Verse 2

```
A            B/A   Am7    D/A    D/G D/A    E6/A  A*
```
Raised by my dad, _____ girl of _____ the day.

```
A         B/A   Am7     D/A    D/G D/A    E6/A  A*
```
He was my man, _____   that was _____ the way.

```
A           B/A    Am7    D/A  D/G D/A    E6/A  A*
```
She was the girl _____ left _____ a-lone.

```
A          B/A    Am7     D/A  D/G    D/A    E6/A  A*
```
Feeling no need _____ to make ___ me ___ her home.

Pre-Chorus 2

```
C          G          Am
```
I don't know what, when or why.

```
C          G          Fmaj7
```
The twilight of love had ar-rived.

Chorus 2   *Repeat Chorus 1*

Interlude   ‖: Am | F/C :‖   *Play 8 times*

Chorus 3   *Repeat Chorus 1*

Outro   ‖: Am E7/B | C6 G/D | E7 | |
             | Am E7/B | C6 G/D | F | :‖ *Play 3 times and fade*

By the Way

Words and Music by Anthony Kiedis,
Flea, John Frusciante and Chad Smith

Melody:

Stand-ing in   line___ to see the

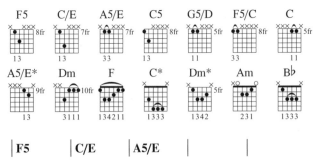

Intro | F5 | C/E | A5/E | |

F5   **C5**   **A5/E**

Chorus 1   Standing in line to see the show tonight and there's a light on, heavy glow.

F5   **C5**   **A5/E**   **G5/D**

By the way, I tried to say I'd be _____ there, waiting for...

F5/C   **C**   **A5/E***

Dani, the girl, is singing songs to me beneath the marquee, overload.

Interlude 1 ||: N.C.(Dm) | :||

N.C.

Verse 1   Steak knife. Card shark.

Con job. Boot cut.

Dm
Skin that flick, she's such a little DJ.

Get there quick by street, but not the freeway.

Turn that trick to make a little leeway.

Beat that nic, but not the way that we play.

Dogtown. Blood bath.

Rib cage. Soft tail.

© 2002 MOEBETOBLAME MUSIC
All Rights Reserved   Used by Permission

| | F | C* | Dm* |
| Chorus 2 | Standing in line to see the show tonight and there's a light on, heavy glow. | | |

| | F | C* | Am | Bb |
| | By the way, I __ tried to say I'd be ___ there, wait-ing for... | | | |

Interlude 2 | N.C.(Dm) | | | |

N.C.

Verse 2   Blackjack. Dope dick.

Pawn shop. Quick pick.

Dm
Kiss that dyke, I know you want to hold one.

Not on strike, but I'm about to bowl one.

Bite that mic, I know you never stole one.

Girls that like a story, so I told one.

Songbird. Main line.

Cash back. Hard top.

	F5	**C/E**	**A5/E**
Chorus 3	Standing in line to see the show tonight and there's a light on, heavy glow.

F5   **C5**   **A5/E**
By the way, I tried to say I'd be _____ there, waiting for...

F5   **C5**
Dani, the girl, is singing songs to me

          A5/E   **G5/D**
Beneath the marquee, oversold.

F5/C   **C**   **A5/E***
By the way, I tried to say I'd be _____ there, waiting for...

Interlude 3 | Dm | | | |

Bridge ||: Dm | :|| *Play 4 times (w/Voc. ad lib.)*
              | |

F   **C***   **Dm***
Chorus 4   Standing in line to see the show tonight and there's a light on, heavy glow.

F   **C***   **Am**   **B♭**
By the way, I ___ tried to say I'd be ___ there, waiting for...

F   **C***
Dani, the girl, is sing-ing songs to me

          Dm*
Beneath the marquee, oversold.

F   **C***   **Am**   **B♭**
By the way, I ___ tried to say I know ___ you from before.

F   **C***   **Dm***
Outro   Standing in line to see the show tonight and there's a light on, heavy glow.

F   **C***   **Am**   **B♭**   **Dm***
By the way, I __ tried to say I'd be ___ there, wait-ing for...

Californication

Words and Music by Anthony Kiedis,
Flea, John Frusciante and Chad Smith

Melody:

Psy-chic spies from _ Chi - na   try   to

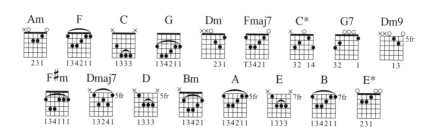

Am	F	C	G	Dm	Fmaj7	C*	G7	Dm9
231	134211	1333	134211	231	T3421	32 14	32 1	13

F#m	Dmaj7	D	Bm	A	E	B	E*
134111	13241	1333	13421	134211	1333	134211	231

Intro   ‖: Am   │F   :‖ ***Play 4 times***

Verse 1
      Am   F
Psychic spies from China try to steal your mind's elation;

      Am   F
Little girls from Sweden dream of silver screen quotations.

         C   G   F   Dm
And if you want these kind of dreams it's Californi-cation.

│Am   │F   │Am   │F   │

Verse 2
            Am   F
It's the   edge of the world and all of western civ'lization;

         Am   F
The sun may rise in the east, at least it settles in the final location.

        C   G   F   Dm
It's understood that Hollywood sells Californi-cation.

Interlude 1   │Am   │Fmaj7   │Am   │Fmaj7   │

© 1999 MOEBETOBLAME MUSIC
All Rights Reserved   Used by Permission

	Am Fmaj7
Pre-Chorus 1	Pay your surgeon very well to break ___ the spell of aging.

      Am   Fmaj7
Ce-lebrity skin, is this your chin, or is ___ that war you're waging?

  Am   Fmaj7 Am   Fmaj7
  First born unicorn,   hardcore soft porn.

  C*   G7   Dm9   Am

Chorus 1   Dream of Cali-fornica - tion,

  C*   G7 Dm9
Dream of Cali-forni-cation.

Interlude 2 | Am | F | Am | F |

  Am   F
Verse 3   Marry me, girl, be my fairy to the world, be my very own constellation;

    Am   F
A teenage bride with a baby inside gettin' high on information.

     C   G   F   Dm
And buy me a star on the boulevard; it's Californi-cation.

| Am | F | Am | F |

  Am   F
Verse 4   Space may be the final frontier, but it's made in a Hollywood basement;

Am   F
Cobain can you hear the spheres singing songs off station to station.

    C   G   F   Dm
And Alderon's not far away; it's Californi-cation.

Interlude 3 | Am | Fmaj7 | Am | Fmaj7 |

  Am   Fmaj7
Pre-Chorus 2 Born and raised by those who praise, con-trol of population.

  Am   Fmaj7
Ev'rybody's been there; I don't ___ mean on vacation.

  Am   Fmaj7 Am   Fmaj7
  First born unicorn,   hardcore soft porn.

Chorus 2

```
C*          G7   Dm9   Am
```
Dream of Cali-fornica - tion.

```
C*          G7   Dm9
```
Dream of Cali-forni-cation.

```
C*          G7   Dm    Am
```
Dream of Cali-fornica - tion.

```
C*          G7   Dm9
```
Dream of Cali-forni-cation.

Guitar Solo

F#m	Dmaj7	F#m	D	
Bm D	A E	F#m	D	
F#m	D	Bm D	A E	
B D	A E	Bm D	A E*	

Interlude 4

Am	F	Am	F	

Verse 5

```
Am                                      F
```
Destruction leads to a very rough road but it also breeds creation;

```
    Am                              F
```
And earthquakes are to a girl's guitar, they're just another good vibration

```
    C              G              F      Dm
```
And tidal waves couldn't save the world from Californi-cation.

Interlude 5

Am	Fmaj7	Am	Fmaj7	

Pre-Chorus 3

```
Am                                  Fmaj7
```
Pay your surgeon very well to break ____ the spell of aging.

```
Am                                    Fmaj7
```
Sicker than the rest, there is no test, but this ____ is what your craving.

```
Am            Fmaj7   Am              Fmaj7
```
   First born unicorn,   hardcore soft porn.

Chorus 3   *Repeat Chorus 2*

Can't Stop

Words and Music by Anthony Kiedis,
Flea, John Frusciante and Chad Smith

Melody:

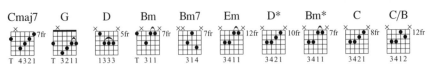

Can't stop, ad-dict - ed to the shin- dig.

Cmaj7   G   D   Bm   Bm7   Em   D*   Bm*   C   C/B

Intro ‖: N.C. | | | :‖
|(E7no3rd) |(Dsus2) |(Bm(add4)) |(Cadd9) |

Verse 1

        N.C.(E7(no3rd))   (Dsus2)
Can't stop, addicted to the shindig.   Chop top, he says I'm gonna win big.

    (Bm(add4))   (Cadd9)
    Choose not a life of imitation,   distant cousin to the reservation.

    (E7(no3rd))   (Dsus2)
    Defunct, the pistol that you pay for.   This punk, the feeling that you stay for.

    (Bm(add4))
    In time I want to be your best friend.

    (Cadd9)
    East side love is living on the west end.

    (E7(no3rd))
    Knocked out, but, boy, you'd better come to.

    (Dsus2)
    Don't die, you know the truth is some do.

    (Bm(add4))
    Go write your message on the pavement.

    (Cadd9)
    Burnin' so bright, I wonder what the wave meant.

    (E7(no3rd))   (Dsus2)
    White heat is screaming in the jungle.   Complete the motion if you stumble.

    (Bm(add4))
    Go ask the dust for any answers.

    Cmaj7
    Come back strong with fifty belly dancers.

© 2002 MOEBETOBLAME MUSIC
All Rights Reserved   Used by Permission

| | G | D | Bm | Cmaj7 |

Chorus 1 The world I love, the tears, I drop to be __ part of the wave, can't stop.

G   D   Bm   Cmaj7
Ever won-der if it's all for you.

   G   D   Bm   Cmaj7
The world I love, the trains I hop to be __ part of the wave, can't stop.

G   D   Bm7 Cmaj7
Come and tell me when it's time   to.

N.C.(E7(no3rd))
Verse 2   Sweetheart is bleeding in the snow cone.

(Dsus2)
So smart, she's leading me to ozone.

(Bm(add4))   (Cadd9)
Music, the great communicator, use two sticks to make it in the nature.

(E7(no3rd))   (Dsus2)
I'll get you into penetration,   the gender of a generation.

(Bm(add4))
The birth of ev'ry other nation.

(Cadd9)
Worth your weight, the gold of meditation.

(E7(no3rd))
This chapter's gonna be a close one.

(Dsus2)
Smoke rings, I know you're gonna blow one.

(Bm(add4))
All on a spaceship, persevering,

(Cadd9)
Use my hands for ev'rything but steering.

(E7(no3rd))
Can't stop the spirits when they need you.

(Dsus2)
Moptops are happy when they feed you.

(Bm(add4))
J. Butterfly is in the treetop.

Cmaj7
Birds that blow the meaning into bebop.

Chorus 2   *Repeat Chorus 1*

Bridge

      Em   **D***   **Bm***
      Wait a minute, I'm passing out, win or lose,

Bm7   **C**   **D***
Just like you.

Em   **C/B** **D***   **Bm***
Far more shocking than an - ything I ever knew.

                C   **D***
How 'bout you.

Em   **D***   **Bm***
Ten more reasons why I ___ need somebody new,

              Cmaj7   **D***
Just like you.

Em   **C/B** **D***   **Bm***
Far more shaking than an - ything I ever knew,

              Cmaj7
Right on cue.

Interlude | **N.C.(E5)** | **(D5)** | **(B5)** | **(C5)** |

Verse 3

N.C.(E7(no3rd))   (Dsus2)
Can't stop, addicted to the shindig.   Chop top, he says I'm gonna win big.

(Bm(add4))   (Cadd9)
Choose not a life of imitation,   distant cousin to the reservation.

(E7(no3rd))
Defunct, the pistol that you pay for.

(Dsus2)
This punk, the feeling that you stay for.

(Bm(add4))
In time I want to be your best friend.

(Cadd9)
East side love is living on the west end.

(E7(no3rd))
Knocked out, but, boy, you'd better come to.

(Dsus2)
Don't die, you know the truth is some do.

(Bm(add4))
Go write your message on the pavement.

(Cadd9)
Burnin' so bright, I wonder what the wave meant.

(E7(no3rd))
Kickstart the golden generator.

(Dsus2)
Sweet-talk, but don't intimidate her.

(Bm(add4))
Can't stop the gods from engineering,

(Cadd9)
Feel no need for any interfering.

(E7(no3rd))   (Dsus2)
Your image in the dictionary,   this life is more than ordinary.

(Bm(add4))
Can I get two, maybe even three of these?

(Cadd9)
Comin' from a space to teach you of the Pleiades.

(E5)
Can't stop the spirits when they need you.

This life is more than just a read-thru.

Catholic School Girls Rule

Words and Music by Anthony Kiedis,
Flea and Cliff Martinez

Melody:

Cath - o - lic   school __ girls rule.

E5

Intro

N.C.(G5)│ (A5) (G5)│ (A5) (G5)│
│ (A5) (C5) (A5) (G5)│
│ (A5) (G5)│ (A5) (G5)│ (A5) (G5)│
│ (A5) (D5) (A5) (G5)│ (A5)

Chorus 1

N.C.(G5) (A5) (G5)   (A5)
    Cath - olic   school girls rule,

(G5) (A5) (C5)   (A5) (G5) (A5)
Cath - olic   school girls rule.

(G5) (A5) (G5)   (A5)
Cath - olic   school girls rule,

(G5) (A5) (D5)   (A5) (G5) (A5)
Cath - olic   school girls rule.

Verse 1

N.C.(B5)
In the class she's taking notes.

Just how deep, deep is my throat?

Mother Mary, don't you know,

She's got eyes like Marylin Monroe.

© 1985 MOEBETOBLAME MUSIC and SCREEN GEMS-EMI MUSIC INC.
All Rights Reserved   Used by Permission

Chorus 2

N.C.(G5) (A5) (G5)   (A5)
    Cath - olic school girls rule,

(G5) (A5) (C5)   (A5) (G5) (A5)
Cath - olic   school girls rule.

(G5) (A5) (G5)   (A5)
Cath - olic   school girls rule,

(G5) (A5) (D5)   (A5) (G5) (A5)
Cath - olic   school girls rule.

(G5) (A5) (G5)   (A5)
Cath - olic   school girls rule,

(G5) (A5) (C5)   (A5) (G5) (A5)
Cath - olic   school girls rule.

(G5) (A5) (G5)   (A5)
Cath - olic   school girls rule,

(G5) (A5) (D5)   (A5) (G5) (A5)
Cath - olic   school girls rule.

Verse 2

N.C.(B5)
From the cross she's raised her head.

This is what the sister said:

Give no love until you wed,

Live no life until you're dead.

Bridge

N.C.(G5)
The good book says we must suppress,

The good book says we must confess.

(A5)
But who cares what the good book says?

Now she's taking off her dress.

Interlude

N.C.(Dm7)				
				E5

Chorus 3   *Repeat Chorus 2*

Verse 3

N.C.(B5)
Lead us not into temptation,

We are pure divine creation.

Talkin' 'bout my generation,

Injected with the seed of emaculation.

(G5) (A5)
Cath - olic.

Coffee Shop

Words and Music by Anthony Kiedis,
Flea, Chad Smith and David Navarro

Melody:

I am just a lous-y bum

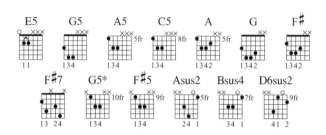

E5   G5   A5   C5   A   G   F#

F#7   G5*   F#5   Asus2   Bsus4   D6sus2

Intro

| N.C. | | | | |
| E5 | G5 | E5 | G5 |

Verse 1

E5   G5
I am just a lousy bum searching for the unknown crumb,

    E5   G5
The crumb, the crumb.

E5
Something or someone to come,

            G5   E5   G5
Come along, illumi-nate my lust. Combust.

    E5
Con-fucius might have been confused

                        G5   E5
And Buddha might have blown a fuse, I ooze the muse.

© 1995 THREE POUNDS OF LOVE MUSIC
All Rights Reserved   Used by Permission

	A5 **G5** **E5**	

Chorus 1

        A5   **G5**   **E5**
Meet me at the ____ coffee shop.

        A5   **C5**   **E5**
   We can dance like ___ Iggy Pop.

        A   **G** **F$\sharp$**   **G**   **F$\sharp$7**
   Another go in the parking lot,

               C5   **A5**
   Frewak the cheek on your hot spot.

Interlude 1   ‖: **E5** | **G5** :‖

             E5

Verse 2   Back and forth my body's jerking,

                        G5   **E5**   **G5**
Will to thrill will not stop working, work and work.

             E5
Take you on a honeymoon,

                       G5   **E5**
Jumpin' on the bed in a hotel room, the room, the groom.

Chorus 2   *Repeat Chorus 1*

Bass Solo 1   ‖: **N.C.(Em7)** | | | :‖

Interlude 2 | **N.C.** | | | |
             | | | | **G5*** **F$\sharp$5 G5***|
             | **N.C.(G$\sharp$5)** | **Asus2** | **Bsus4** | **D6sus2** |

Chorus 3   *Repeat Chorus 1*

Bass Solo 2   ‖: **E5** | | | :‖ *Play 4 times*

Don't Forget Me

Words and Music by Anthony Kiedis,
Flea, John Frusciante and Chad Smith

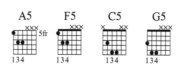

A5   F5   C5   G5

Intro   ‖: A5   F5 | C5   G5   :‖

Verse 1
A5   F5
   I'm an ocean   in your bedroom,

C5   G5   A5
   Make ya feel warm. Make you want to reassume.

                    F5   C5   G5
Now we know ____ it all ____ for sure.

A5   F5
   I'm a dance hall,   dirty break beat,

C5   G5   A5
   Make the snow fall up from underneath your feet.

                F5 C5   G5   A5
Not alone,   I'll be there. Tell ____ me when you wanna go.

Interlude 1   ‖: A5   F5 | C5   G5   :‖

© 2002 MOEBETOBLAME MUSIC
All Rights Reserved   Used by Permission

Verse 2

```
A5                  F5
I'm a meth lab,    first rehab,

C5                  G5                      A5
Take it all off and step inside the running cab.

            F5          C5      G5
There's a love ___ that knows ___ the way.

A5                  F5
I'm the rainbow      in your jail cell,

C5                  G5                          A5
All the memories of ev'rything you've ever smelled.

       F5  C5              G5
Not alone,     I'll be there. Tell ___ me when you wanna go.
```

Chorus 1

```
A5      F5      C5      G5
Oh, _____ oh.

A5                  F5
Don't forget me, I can't hide it.

C5                  G5
Come again, get me excited.
```

Guitar Solo

```
‖: A5      F5    | C5      G5      :‖
```

Verse 3

```
A5                  F5
I'm an inbred      and a pothead,

C5                  G5                      A5
Two legs that you spread inside the tool shed.

            F5      C5      G5
Now we know ___ it all ___ for sure.

A5                  F5
I could show you     to the free field,

C5              G5                          A5
Overcome and more will always be revealed.

       F5  C5              G5
Not alone,      I'll be there. Tell ___ me when you wanna go.
```

	A5 F5 C5 G5
Chorus 2	Oh, _____ and...

| A5   F5 |
| Don't forget me, I can't hide it. |

| C5   G5 |
| Come again, get me excited. |

| A5   F5 C5 G5 |
| Oh, oh, _____ and... |

| A5   F5 |
| Don't forget me, I can't hide it. |

| C5   G5 |
| Grab a match, now let me light it. |

| *Interlude 2* | ‖: A5   F5 | C5   G5   :‖   *Play 4 times* |

	A5 F5
Verse 4	I'm the blood stain on your shirt sleeve

| C5   G5   A5 |
| Coming down and more ____ are coming to believe. |

| F5   C5   G5 |
| Now we know ____ it all ____ for sure. |

| A5   F5 |
| Make the hair stand   up on your arm, |

| C5   G5   A5 |
| Teach you how to dance ____ inside the funny farm. |

| F5 C5   G5   A5   F5 |
| Not alone,   I'll be there. Tell ____ me when you wanna go. |

| C5   G5   A5   F5 |
| I'll be there to tell ____ me when you wanna go. |

| C5   G5   A5   F5 |
| Come again and tell ____ me when you wanna go. |

| C5   G5   A5   F5 |
| More will be re-vealed, my friend. |

Easily

Words and Music by Anthony Kiedis,
Flea, John Frusciante and Chad Smith

Melody:

Eas - i - ly, _____

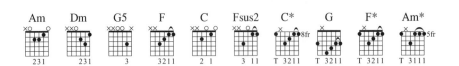

Intro

|Am   Dm| G5 |F   C Am| |

Verse 1

Am Dm F   C   Am
Easi - ly,   let's get car-ried a-way.

    Dm F   C   Am
Easi-ly,   let's get mar-ried to-day.

                  Dm
Shao Lin shouted a rose from his throat.

F   C   Am
   Ev'rything must go.

                   Dm
A lickin' stick is thicker when you break it to show.

Fsus2   C   Am
   Ev'rything must go.

Chorus 1

        C*   G   F*
The story of a woman on the morning of a war.

        C*   G   F*
Re-mind me, if you will, exactly what we're fighting for.

Am*   G   F*
Calling, calling for something in the air.

Am*   G   F*
Calling, calling I know you must be there.

© 1999 MOEBETOBLAME MUSIC
All Rights Reserved   Used by Permission

Verse 2

                    Am Dm F   C   Am
                    Easi - ly,   let's get caught in a wave.

                        Dm F   C   Am
                    Easi-ly,   we won't get caught in a cage.

                                        Dm
                    Shao Lin shakin' for the sake of his soul.

                    F   C   Am
                      Ev'rything must go.

                                        Dm
                    Lookin' mighty tired of all the things that you own.

                    Fsus2   C   Am
                      Ev'rything must go.

Chorus 2

                    C*   G   F*
                    I can't tell you who to idol-ize.

                        C*   G   F*
                    You think it's almost over but it's only on the rise.

                    Am*   G   F*
                    Calling, calling for something in the air.

                    Am*   G   F*
                    Calling, calling I know you must be there.

Chorus 3

                        C*   G   F*
                    The story of a woman on the morning of a war.

                        C*   G   F*
                    Re-mind me, if you will, exactly what we're fighting for.

                    Am*   G   F*
                    Throw me to the wolves because there's order in the pack.

                    Am*   G   F*
                    Throw me to the sky because I know I'm coming back.

| **Guitar Solo** | ‖: Am   Dm | | |F   C Am| | :‖ |

Verse 3

Am   Dm
Shao Lin shakin' for the sake of his soul.

F   C   Am
  Ev'rything must go.

                  Dm
Lookin' mighty tired of all the things that you own.

Fsus2   C   Am
  Ev'rything must go.

Chorus 4

     C*   G   F*
The story of a woman on the morning of a war.

     C*   G   F*
Re-mind me, if you will, exactly what we're fighting for.

Am*   G   F*
Calling, calling for something in the air.

Am*   G   F*
Calling, calling I know you must be there.

Chorus 5

C*   G   F*
I don't want to be your little research monkey boy.

     C*   G   F*
The creature that I am is only going to de-stroy.

Am*   G   F*
Throw me to the wolves because there's order in the pack.

Am*   G   F*
Throw me to the sky because I know I'm coming back.

Outro

‖: C* |G   F* |C* |G   F* |
|Am* |G   F* |Am* |G   F* :‖ *Play 3 times*
| N.C.(C)

Fight Like a Brave

Words and Music by Anthony Kiedis,
Flea, Hillel Slovak and Jack Irons

Melody:

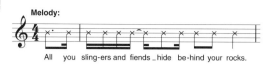

All you sling-ers and fiends _ hide be-hind your rocks.

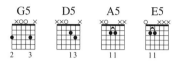

G5   D5   A5   E5

Intro | N.C.(Am7) | | | **G5 D5** |

                  N.C.(Am7)

Verse 1   *All you slingers and fiends hide behind your rocks.*

                                            G5   D5

Put down your guard, I'm not here to box.

             N.C.(Am7)

This is no showdown, so throw down your guns.

You see it doesn't matter where you come from.

You could be from Park Ave or from a park bench,

                           G5   **D5**

You could be a politician or a bitchy prin-cess.

             N.C.(Am7)

But if you're lookin' for a fist and you're lookin' to unite,

Put your knuckleheads together; make a fist and fight.

Not to your death and not to your grave.

                           G5   **D5**

I'm talkin' 'bout that freedom. Fight like a brave.

© 1987 MOEBETOBLAME MUSIC and SCREEN GEMS-EMI MUSIC INC.
All Rights Reserved   Used by Permission

Chorus 1 N.C.(Bm7)
Fight like a brave. Don't be a slave.

                                   A5   E5
No one can tell you you've got to be a-fraid.

Interlude 1 | N.C.(Am7) | | | G5 D5 |

Verse 2 N.C.(Am7)
If you're sick-a-sick 'n' tired of being sick and tired, uh,

                                   G5   D5
If you're sick of all the bullshit and you're sick of all the lies,

N.C.(Am7)
It's better late than never to set-a-set it straight.

You know the lie is dead so give yourself a break.

Get it through your head and get it off your chest.

                   G5   D5
Get it out your arm because it's time to start fresh.

N.C.(Am7)
You want to stop dying the life you could be livin'.

I'm here to tell a story but I'm also here to listen.

No, I'm not your preacher and I'm not your physician.

                   G5   D5
I'm just trying to reach you; I'm a rebel with a mission.

Chorus 2 N.C.(Bm7)
Fight like a brave. Don't be a slave.

No one can tell you you've got to be afraid.

Fight like a brave. Don't be a slave.

                                   A5   E5   A5   E5
No one can tell you you've got to be a-fraid.

Interlude 2

N.C.(E5)
I am here today to talk about the uplift mofo party plan.

A plan based on a band, a band based on a plan.

There should be no slaves in the land of lands. It's a Hollywood town.

Guitar Solo

‖:N.C.(E5) | | | :‖
| | | G5 D5 |

Verse 3

N.C.(Am7)
You say you're running and you're running and you're running afraid.

G5   D5
You say you ran across the planet but you couldn't get away.

N.C.(Am7)
The fire in your brain was driving you insane.

You were looking for a day in a life that never came.

So don't tell me that I've got to take a number

G5   D5
'Cause I've been to that doctor and be-lieve me, that's a bummer.

N.C.(Am7)
Here's a one of a kind convention of the mind,

And don't forget to mention that it doesn't cost a dime.

Come as you like and leave any time.

G5   D5
And one more thing: You know it doesn't have to rhyme.

Chorus 3

N.C.(Am7)
‖: Fight like a brave. (Ah, like a brave.) Don't be a slave. (I'm no slave.)

G5   D5
No one can tell you you've got to be a-fraid.   :‖ ***Repeat and fade***

Fortune Faded

Words and Music by Anthony Kiedis,
Flea, John Frusciante and Chad Smith

Melody:

They say in chess _ you've got to kill ____ the queen and

F# D A A* G Bm Bm7

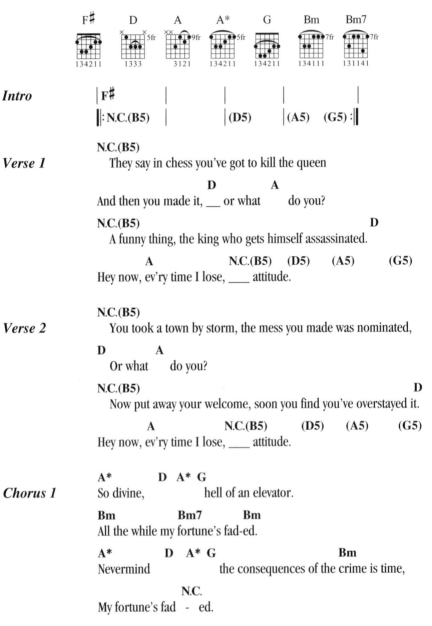

Intro

```
| F#        |          |          |          |
||: N.C.(B5) |          | (D5)     | (A5)  (G5) :||
```

Verse 1

N.C.(B5)
They say in chess you've got to kill the queen

                 D   A
And then you made it, ___ or what   do you?

N.C.(B5)   D
A funny thing, the king who gets himself assassinated.

       A   N.C.(B5)   (D5)   (A5)   (G5)
Hey now, ev'ry time I lose, ____ attitude.

Verse 2

N.C.(B5)
You took a town by storm, the mess you made was nominated,

D   A
Or what   do you?

N.C.(B5)   D
Now put away your welcome, soon you find you've overstayed it.

       A   N.C.(B5)   (D5)   (A5)   (G5)
Hey now, ev'ry time I lose, ____ attitude.

Chorus 1

A*   D   A*   G
So divine,   hell of an elevator.

Bm   Bm7   Bm
All the while my fortune's fad-ed.

A*   D   A*   G   Bm
Nevermind   the consequences of the crime is time,

                 N.C.
My fortune's fad - ed.

© 2001 MOEBETOBLAME MUSIC
All Rights Reserved   Used by Permission

Interlude	‖: N.C.(B5)	|(D5) |(A5) (G5) :‖

Verse 3

N.C.(B5)   D
    The medicated state of mind you found is overrated,

       A
Or what   do you?

N.C.(B5)   D
    You saw it all come down and now it's time to imitate it.

        A   N.C.(B5)   (D5)   (A5)   (G5)
Hey now, ev'ry time I lose,   attitude.

Chorus 2   *Repeat Chorus 1*

Bridge

| N.C.(B5) | |(D5) |(A5)   (G5) |

N.C.(B5)   (D5)   (A5)   (G5)
Come on, God, do I seem bulletproof?

| F♯ | | | | |

Chorus 3

A*   D A* G
So divine, _____ hell of an elevator.

Bm   Bm7   Bm
All the while my fortune's fad-ed.

A*   D A* G   Bm
Nevermind   the consequences of the crime is time,

Bm7   Bm
My fortune's fad-ed.

A*   D A* G
So divine,   hell of an elevator.

Bm   Bm7   Bm
All the while my fortune's fad-ed.

A*   D A* G   Bm
Nevermind   the consequences of the crime is time,

        N.C.
My for - tune's faded.

Funky Monks

Words and Music by Anthony Kiedis,
Flea, John Frusciante and Chad Smith

Melody:

There are no __ monks in my band. __

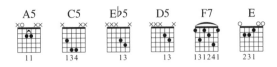

A5 C5 Eb5 D5 F7 E

Intro   ‖: N.C.(G) | | | :‖

Verse 1

N.C.(G)
There are no monks in my band. (There are no monks in my band.)

There are no saints in me land. (There are no saints in me land.)

I'll be doin' all I can, if I die an honest man. (If I die an honest man.)

Confusion is my middle name. (Confusion is my middle name.)

Ask me again, I'll tell you the same. (Ask me again, I'll tell you the same.)

Persuaded by one sexy dame. No, I do not feel no shame.

Chorus 1

A5   C5   Eb5   D5   F7   E
(You are __ on ___ the ___ road.)

A5   C5   Eb5   D5
Can I get a little lovin' from you,

    F7   E
Can I get a little bit of that done did do?

A5   C5   Eb5   D5   F7   E
(You are __ on ___ the ___ road.)

A5   C5   Eb5   D5
Tell me now, girl, did you need me too? Aw!

N.C.(A5)   N.C.
Tell me now, girl, 'cause I've got a feeling for you.

© 1991 MOEBETOBLAME MUSIC
All Rights Reserved   Used by Permission

Verse 2

N.C.(G)
Ev'ry man has certain needs. (Ev'ry man has certain needs.)

Talkin' 'bout them dirty deeds. (Talkin' 'bout them dirty deeds.)

To these needs I must concede, livin' by my lowly creed.

(Livin' by my lowly creed.)

A woman please know that I'm good.

(A woman please know that I'm good.)

Know that I did all I could. (Know that I did all I could.)

But, yes, it's true the likelihood, yeah, yeah, of being great is not so good.

Chorus 2   *Repeat Chorus 1*

Guitar Solo   ‖: N.C.(B5) | | | :‖
                   ‖: N.C.(D5) | | | :‖

Verse 3

N.C.(G)
There are no monks in my band. (There are no monks in my band.)

There are no saints in this land. (There are no saints in this land.)

I'll be doin' all I can if I die an honest man. (If I die an honest man.)

Virtue slipped into my shoe. (Virtue slipped into my shoe.)

No, I will not misconstrue. (No, I will not misconstrue.)

More rockin', more rockin', now, doobley do, yeah, yeah.

Dancin' down your avenue.

Chorus 3   *Repeat Chorus 1*

Outro   ‖: N.C.(B) | | | :‖ *Play 6 times and fade*

Get on Top

Words and Music by Anthony Kiedis,
Flea, John Frusciante and Chad Smith

Melody:

Get on top.

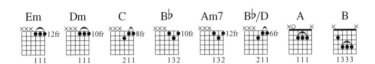

Em   Dm   C   B♭   Am7   B♭/D   A   B

Intro | N.C.(Em) | | | |

Get on top.   *Get on top.*

| | | | |

Hit me, *come get me.* *I bite but* *she bit me.*

Verse 1

N.C.(Em)
Gorilla, cunttilla, Sammy D. and a salmonella.

Come with me 'cause I'm an ass killer; you're ill but I'm iller.

I'll malinger on your block and give the finger to a cop

And pick a lock before I knock and set you up to get on top.

Chorus 1 | N.C.(Am) | | |

Complications of a mastermind,

Last temptation of my kind.

Extra planetary sign, when do we align?

                    Em
All in time,   right on.

© 1999 MOEBETOBLAME MUSIC
All Rights Reserved   Used by Permission

Interlude 1 | N.C.(Em) | | |
                           Get up,   a, come sit up.   Oh, I light but   she lit up. |

Verse 2   N.C.(Em)
Grasshopper, show stopper, the life of a wife swapper.

Come with me 'cause I'm a big bopper; you do but I wopper.

Exterminate my cause, you want to draw some straws,

Be the one to see my flaws, make me bleed with painted claws.

Chorus 2   *Repeat Chorus 1*

Guitar Solo   ‖:Dm | | C | :‖
Bb	Am7	Bb	Am7
Dm		Bb/D	C
Dm	Em	Bb	C
A	B

Interlude 2   *Repeat Intro*

Verse 3   N.C.(Em)
Speedballer, Rhodes scholar, bottom bitch and a bottom dollar.

Come with me 'cause I'm a free faller; you hoot but I holler.

I'll malinger on your block and give the finger to a cop and

Pick a lock before I knock on. Set you up to get on top.

Outro   ‖: N.C.(Em) | :‖ *Play 4 times*
                              Get on top.

Get Up and Jump

Words and Music by
Anthony Kiedis and Flea

Melody:

A get up an' jump, a get up an' jump. A

E13   A7

Intro   ‖: E13 | | | :‖
            | N.C.(G5) | | |

Verse 1

N.C.(G5)
A get up an' jump, a get up an' jump. A get up, get up, get up an' jump.

A jump on up, a jump on down,

Just jump a, jump a, jump a, jump a, jump around.

Jump the day away, jump all over town

'Cause jumpin's okay in a jumpin' kinda way. Hey, hey.

Jump a boy, jump a girl, jump a rope, jump for joy.

Just don't stop jumpin', keep your heart muscle pumpin'.

Hillel be jumpin' on that little baby Frumpkin.

Say, what you got, a pumpkin in your pants?

When you're just standin' or sittin' still, think about the frogs gettin' a thrill.

Take a little lesson from the kangaroos,

A don't you know they're jumpin' frogs. Jump you.

Jump a nun, jump a jack, jump for fun, jump back.

A how's about us jumpin' in the sack? A now it's time for a jump attack.

© 1984 MOEBETOBLAME MUSIC
All Rights Reserved   Used by Permission

	A7
Chorus 1	Get up an' jump. Get up an' jump.

Get up an' jump. Get up an' jump.

Get up an' jump, jump. Get up an' jump.

Get up an' jump. Get up an' jump.

Interlude 1 | N.C.(G5)　　　|　　　　　|　　　　　|　　　　　|

N.C.(G5)

Verse 2 *Jama bora, jima bora, slima bora boogie*

To the tune of Slima Billy; lookin' like you're mighty silly.

(Say what?) You got a pumpkin in your pants?

(Say what?) You got a pumpkin in your pants?

A mister Mexican jumping bean knows his fun is squeaky clean.

Christ, how'd ya think that he got so clean.

Not from sittin' on his goddamn spleen. Get up.

Oh, I be jumpin', I be jumpin', I be jumpin' alone.

I be jumpin' for the phone, I be jumpin' Misses Jones.

I really want to jump on Kinski's bones.

	A7
Chorus 2	Get up an' jump. Get up an' jump.

Get up an' jump. Get up an' jump.

Get up an' jump, jump. Get up an' jump.

Get up an' jump. Get up an' jump.

Get up an' jump. Get up an' jump.

Get up an' jump. Get up an' jump.

Get up an' jump. Get up an' jump.

Get up an' jump. Get up an' jump.

Interlude 2 | **N.C.(G5)** | | | |

N.C.(G5)

Verse 3 *Jama bora, jima bora, slima bora boogie*

To the tune of Slima Billy, lookin' like you're mighty silly.

(Say what?) You got a pumpkin in your pants?

(Say what?) You got a pumpkin in your pants?

Outro | **E13** | | | |

Give It Away

Words and Music by Anthony Kiedis,
Flea, John Frusciante and Chad Smith

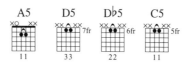

Intro | N.C.(A5) | | | |

Verse 1   N.C.(A5)
What I've got, you've got to give it to your mama.

What I've got, you've got to give it to your papa.

What I've got, you've got to give it to your daughter,

Then you do a little dance, and then you drink a little water.

What I've got, you've got to get it, put it in you.

What I've got, you've got to get it, put it in you.

What I've got, you've got to get it, put it in you.

Reeling with the feeling, don't stop, continue.

Realize I don't wanna be a miser,

Confide with Sly, you'll be the wiser.

Young blood is the lovin' upriser.

How come ev'rybody wanna keep it like the Kaiser?

© 1991 MOEBETOBLAME MUSIC
All Rights Reserved   Used by Permission

Chorus 1

N.C.(A5)
Give it away, give it away, give it away now.

Give it away, give it away, give it away now.

Give it away, give it away, give it away now.

I can't tell if I'm a kingpin or a pauper!

Verse 2

N.C.(A5)
Greedy little people in a sea of distress,

Keep your move to receive your less.

Unimpressed by material excess,

Love is free, love me, say "Hell yes!"

Low brow, but I rock a little know how.

No time for the piggies or the hoosegow.

Get smart, get down with the power,

Never been a better time than right now.

Bob Marley, poet and a prophet,

Bob Marley taught me how to off it.

Bob Marley walkin' like he talk it.

Goodness me, can't you see I'm gonna cough it?

Chorus 2	N.C.(A5) Give it away, give it away, give it away now.
	Give it away, give it away, give it away now.
	Give it away, give it away, give it away now. Oh, oh, yeah!
	Give it away, give it away, give it away now.
	Give it away, give it away, give it away now.
	Give it away, give it away, give it away now.
	I can't tell if I'm a kingpin or a pauper!
Guitar Solo 1	‖: N.C.(E5) | | | :‖
Verse 3	N.C.(A5) Lucky me, swimmin' in my ability,
	Dancin' down on life with agility.
	Come and drink it up from my fertility,
	Blessed with a bucket of lucky mobility.
	My mom, I love her 'cause she love me,
	Long gone are the times when she scrub me.
	Feelin' good, my brother gonna hug me,
	Drink up my juice, young love, chug-a-lug me.
	There's a river born to be a giver,
	Keep you warm, won't let you shiver.
	His heart is never gonna wither,
	Come on ev'rybody, time to deliver.

Chorus 3   *Repeat Chorus 1*

Guitar Solo 2 | N.C.(E5) | | | |

Verse 4   *Repeat Verse 1*

Chorus 4

N.C.(A5)
    Give it away, give it away, give it away now.

Give it away, give it away, give it away now.

Give it away, give it away, give it away now.

Give it away, give it away, give it away now.

Give it away now. Give it away now.

Outro

N.C.(A5)
‖:   Give it away now.   :‖ *Play 10 times*

   A5   D5 D♭5 C5
‖:   Give it away now.   :‖ *Play 8 times*

A5
   Give it away   now.

Good Time Boys

Words and Music by Anthony Kiedis,
Flea, John Frusciante and Chad Smith

Melody:

In - deed it may seem that we have strange ways, but we

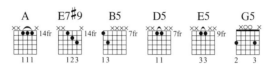

A   E7#9   B5   D5   E5   G5

Intro | N.C.(Em7) | | | **A** |

Hey, yeah!

‖: **E7#9** | **A**   :‖   ***Play 4 times***

          E7#9
Verse 1   *In-deed it may seem that we have strange ways,*

    But we do it with compassion and don't believe in age.

    Travel 'round the world gettin' naked on the stage,

                     A
    Bustin' people out of their ev'ryday cage.

      E7#9   **A**   **E7#9**   **A**
    Well, we like to think we make a sad man happy,

       E7#9   **A**   **E7#9**   **A**
    And we like to make proud   our mammy and our pappy.

    E7#9
    Funky young kings, we sing of truth and soul.

    We're the modern day braves with one strong hold.

    Through the world of song our boldness is exposed.

          N.C.
    Talkin' 'bout my buddies, funk it up Fishbone.

© 1989 MOEBETOBLAME MUSIC
All Rights Reserved Used by Permission

Interlude 1	| E7#9 | A | E7#9 | |

                 Hey, hey.

                B5   **D5 E5**   **D5 E5**

Chorus 1   Good, good time boys, make me feel good.

                B5   **D5 E5 G5**

                Give me good times, yea, yea, yea, yea.

                B5   **D5 E5**   **D5 E5**

                Good, good time boys, make me feel good.

                B5   **D5 E5 G5**

                Give me good times, yea, yea, yea, yea.

Interlude 2	| E7#9 | | | A |

                  E7#9

Verse 2   *Our de-votion to emotion is more than evident.*

                To the minds that are open, it's you we represent.

                We hope you have enjoyed the time that you have spent,

                                    A

                One day the good time boys might jest be president,

                  E7#9   **A**   **E7#9**   **A**

                Like a pack of mad hatters,   *who come from outer space.*

                  E7#9   **A**   **E7#9**   **A**

                Our swingin's gonna shatter   *ev'ry stone cold face.*

                  E7#9

                Now you may not know the exact reason why,

                A band commands attention from the mountains and the sky.

                Makin' more than money, more than money can buy,

                I stop! and take a listen to the Monsters try.

Interlude 3   *Repeat Interlude 1*

Chorus 2   *Repeat Chorus 1*

Interlude 4	**E7♯9**			**N.C.**	
				Got me bonin'...	
	N.C.(G7)				

E7♯9

Verse 3   *If you don't believe me you can ask John Doe,*

'Cause his heart is made of glory and his voice is made of gold.

He'll tell you in a minute about the men he knows,

                              A
He'll tell you 'bout the band called FIREHOSE.

   E7♯9   **A**   **E7♯9**   **A**
To those of you who doubt   the nature of our spirit,

   E7♯9   **A**   **E7♯9**   **A**
We play it out loud __ for everyone to hear it.

     E7♯9
B-B-B-Building up our brains with supernatural powers,

We take it from the trees and the mighty Watts Towers.

Aim the flame of freedom at the lames and sours,

               N.C.
We're the best of the West and the West is ours.

Interlude 5 | **E7♯9** | | | |

Chorus 3   *Repeat Chorus 1*

Chorus 4   *Repeat Chorus 1*

             E7♯9
Outro   ‖: Rockin' freakopotamus, rockin' freakopotamus. :‖ *Play 7 times*

Higher Ground

Words and Music
by Stevie Wonder

Melody:

Peo - ple, _____

| E5 | G5 | A5 | F#5 | B5 | D5 | E5* | G5* | A5* |

Intro   ‖: E5   G5   A5 | E5   G5   A5   :‖   *Play 4 times*

Verse 1

E5   G5 A5 E5 G5   A5 E5   G5 A5   E5   G5 A5
People,   keep on ___ learnin'.

E5   G5 A5 E5 G5   A5 E5   G5 A5   E5   G5 A5
Soldiers,   keep on ___ warrin'.

    F#5   A5 B5 F#5   A5   B5 A5
Uh, world, _____ keep on ___ turnin',

D5   E5   G5 A5
    'Cause it won't be too long.

| E5   G5 A5 | E5   G5 A5 | E5   G5 A5 |

Verse 2

      E5   G5 A5 E5   G5   A5 E5   G5 A5   E5 G5
Uh, powers _____   a keep on ___ lyin',

A5   E5   G5 A5 E5
While your people

    G5   A5 E5   G5 A5   E5 G5 A5
A keep on ___ dyin'.

    F#5   A5 B5 F#5   A5   B5 A5
Uh, world, _____   keep on ___ turnin',

D5   E5   G5 A5
    'Cause it won't be too long.

| E5   G5 A5 | E5   G5 A5 | E5   G5 A5 |

© 1973 (Renewed 2001) JOBETE MUSIC CO., INC. and BLACK BULL MUSIC
c/o EMI APRIL MUSIC INC.
All Rights Reserved   International Copyright Secured   Used by Permission

     A5   E5
Chorus 1 I'm so darn glad he let me try it again,

       A5   E5
     'Cause my last time on earth I lived a whole world of sin.

     A5   E5
     I'm so glad that I know more than I knew then.

      F#5   B5   E5   G5 A5
     Gonna keep on tryin' till ____ I reach the highest ground.

     | E5 G5 A5 | E5 G5 A5 | E5 G5 A5 |

      E5   G5 A5 E5 G5   A5 E5   G5 A5 E5 G5 A5
Verse 3 Uh, teachers, ____   a keep on ____ teachin'.

      E5   G5 A5 E5
     Uh, preachers, _____

      G5   A5 E5   G5 A5 E5 G5 A5
     A keep on ____ preachin'.

     F#5 A5 B5 F#5 A5   B5 A5
     World, _____ keep on ____ turnin',

     D5   E5 G5 A5
      'Cause it won't be too long.

     | E5 G5 A5 | E5 G5 A5 | E5 G5 A5 |
          Oh, no.

      E5   G5 A5 E5 G5   A5 E5   G5 A5 E5 G5
Verse 4 Lovers, _____   a keep on ____ lovin',

     A5   E5   G5 A5 E5   G5 A5 E5   G5 A5 E5 G5 A5
     While be-lievers ____   keep on be - lievin'.

     F#5 A5 B5 F#5 A5   B5 A5
     Sleepers, _____ just stop ____ sleepin',

     D5   E5 G5 A5
      'Cause it won't be too long.

     | E5 G5 A5 | E5 G5 A5 | E5 G5 A5 |
          Oh, no!

Chorus 2   *Repeat Chorus 1*

Outro

| | G5 | A5 | E5 | G5 | A5 | E5 | G5 A5 |

An' __ Stevie knows that, uh, nobody's __ gonna bring me down.

    E5   **G5**   **A5**   **E5**

Till __ I reach ___ the highest ground.

G5   **A5**   **E5**

'Cause me 'n' Stevie, see,

            G5 A5   **E5**   **G5**   **A5**

We're gonna be a sailin' on __ the get funky sound.

    E5   **G5**   **A5**   **E5**

Till ___ I reach ___ the highest ground.

         G5 A5   **E5**   **G5 A5**   **E5 G5**   **A5**

Bustin' out, ___ an' I'll break you out, ___ 'cause I'm   *sailin' on.*

    E5   **G5**   **A5**   **E5**

Till ___ I reach ___ the highest ground.

G5 A5 E5   **G5 A5**   **E5**   **G5**   **A5**

Just, uh, ___ sailin' on, ___ sail-in' on the high-er ground.

    E5   **E5***   **G5* A5* G5* E5***   **G5***   **A5***   **G5***

Till ___ I reach the highest ground.

‖: **E5*** | **G5*A5* G5*** | **E5*** | **G5*A5* G5*** :‖ **E5***

If You Have to Ask

Words and Music by Anthony Kiedis,
Flea, John Frusciante and Chad Smith

Melody:

A wan-na-be gang-ster think-in' he's a wise guy,

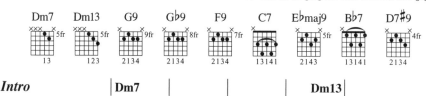

Dm7   Dm13   G9   Gb9   F9   C7   Ebmaj9   Bb7   D7#9

Intro |Dm7 | | | Dm13|

Verse 1

Dm7
A wannabe gangster thinkin' he's a wise guy,

Rob another bank, he's a sock 'em in the eye guy.

Tank head, Mister Bonnie and Clyde guy,
                                       Dm13
Look him in the eye, he is not my kinda guy.
Dm7
Never wanna be confusion,

Prefer pudding sweet, but too aloofer.

Orange eyed girl with a backslide dew said,
                     Dm13
"Yo, homie, who you talkin' to?"
Dm7
Backed up paddy wagon, mackin' on a cat's ass,

One upper cut to the cold, upper middle class.

Born to storm on boredom's face,
                         Dm13
Add a little lust to the funky ass Flea bass.
Dm7
Most in the race just lose their grace,

The blackest hole in all of space.

Crooked as a hooker, now, suck my thumb,
                     Dm13
Anybody wanna come get some?

© 1991 MOEBETOBLAME MUSIC
All Rights Reserved   Used by Permission

Chorus 1	N.C.(C5) (If you have to ask,) you'll never know.
	Funky mother fucker will not be told to go.
	(If you have to ask,) you'll never know.
	Funky mother fucker will not be told to go-o-o-o.
Interlude 1	*Repeat Intro*
Verse 2	Dm7 *Don't ask me why I'm flyin' so high.*
	Mister Bubble meets Super Fly in my third eye.

	Searchin' for a soul bride, she's my freakette,
	                              Dm13
	Soak it up inside, deeper than a secret.
	Dm7
	  Much more than meets the eye,

	To the funk I fall into my new ride.
	My hand, my hand,
	Dm13 *Magic on the one is a medicine man.* Dm7 *Thinkin' of a few taboos that I ought to kill,*
	Dancin' on a face like a stage in Vaudeville.
	I feel so good, can't be understood, Dm13 *Booty of a hoodlum rockin' my red hood.*
Chorus 2	*Repeat Chorus 1*
Interlude 2	‖: G9 G♭9 F9 C7 | E♭maj9 B♭7 D7#9 :‖ *Play 4 times*
Guitar Solo	‖: Dm7 | | | Dm13 :‖ *Play 4 times* | N.C.(D5) | |
Outro	| Dm7 | | | Dm13 | | Dm7 | | | |

Johnny Kick a Hole in the Sky

Words and Music by Anthony Kiedis,
Flea, John Frusciante and Chad Smith

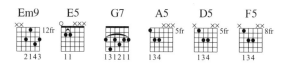

| Em9 | E5 | G7 | A5 | D5 | F5 |

Intro

Em9
I, I, I, I, I, I, I, I, I, I, I, I

E5
Cry, I cry!

Verse 1

Em9
I was born in a land. I don't think you understand,

E5
God damn, what I am.

Em9
I'm a native of this place, please don't kick me in my face.

E5
My race has been disgraced.

Pre-Chorus 1

E5
Pow, pow!

Sing it again y'all.

Pow, pow!

© 1989 MOEBETOBLAME MUSIC
All Rights Reserved   Used by Permission

Chorus 1

G7
Won't somebody testify, kick a hole right in the sky.
A5
(Testify, testify, kick a hole right in the sky.)
G7
Slap a liar in his eye, kick a hole right in the sky.
A5
(Testify, testify, kick a hole right in the sky.)
D5   F5
Johnny, Johnny, Johnny.
Em9
  I, I, I, I, I, I, I, I, I wonder why, a why.

Verse 2

Em9
Put us in your pumpkin shell, where you keep us very well.
E5
It's hell, where I dwell.
Em9
When hist'ry books are full of shit, I'll become the anarchist.
E5
I'm pissed at this.
Em9
What this country came to be, it's a lie,
E5
No place for me. I bleed.

Pre-Chorus 2   *Repeat Pre-Chorus 1*

Chorus 2

G7
Won't somebody testify, kick a hole right in the sky.
A5
(Testify, testify, kick a hole right in the sky.)
G7
Slap a liar in his eye, kick a hole right in the sky.
A5
(Testify, testify, kick a hole right in the sky.)
D5   F5
Johnny, Johnny, Johnny.
Em9   E5
  I, I, I, I, I, I, I, I, I de-cide to defy.

Verse 3

Em9
Kill my trust, if you must, but in my blood

     E5
There is the lust for life. That's right.

  Em9
A-pache blood is in my heart dashing through me like a shark.

E5
Crashing through the dark.

Pre-Chorus 3   *Repeat Pre-Chorus 1*

Chorus 3

G7
Won't somebody testify, kick a hole right in the sky.

A5
(Testify, testify, kick a hole right in the sky.)

G7
Slap a liar in his eye, kick a hole right in the sky.

A5
(Testify, testify, kick a hole right in the sky.)

D5   F5
Johnny, Johnny, Johnny.

Em9   E5
 I, I, I, I, I, I, I, I, I de-fy to confide.

Verse 4

Em9
What am I supposed to do, I feel like I'm cut in two?

  E5
Con-fused by rules.

Em9
Do these two cultures clash or am I living in the past?

  E5
I ask. Please tell me fast.

Pre-Chorus 4   *Repeat Pre-Chorus 1*

RED HOT CHILI PEPPERS

Chorus 4

G7
Won't somebody testify, kick a hole right in the sky.
A5
(Testify, testify, kick a hole right in the sky.)
G7
Slap a liar in his eye, kick a hole right in the sky.
A5
(Testify, testify, kick a hole right in the sky.)
D5   F5
Johnny, Johnny, Johnny.
Em9   E5
  I, I, I, I, I, I, I, I, I, I, I. That's right.

Verse 5

Em9
  To what do I belong, an' if I change will I be wrong,
  E5
Be wrong, just wrong?
 Em9
I took my foot an' kicked a hole in the sky.
   E5
I pro-ceeded to plead, "Will Fathers help me decide?"
 Em9
A jagged flash of light struck me in the eye.
 E5
I turned around an' found that I was still alive.
  Em9
Snakes rise high from the purple black sky.
  E5
The red cloud rains an' the black horse rides.
    Em9
Then it dawned on me like the mornin' sun,
   E5
I'm a part of two worlds and the mornin' comes.
Em9
Glowing embers tend to remember when
  E5
The power that is peace was treated as a friend.
   Em9
I'm a master of objection an' I got to take action,
  E5
I'm a man. The animal man.

Outro

| E5 | | | | |

Jungle Man

Words and Music by Anthony Kiedis,
Flea, Cliff Martinez and Jack Sherman

Melody:

Deep in - side the

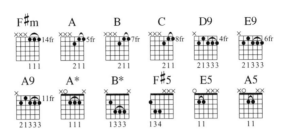

Intro | N.C.(F#5) (E5) |(F#5) (E5) (F#5) | (E5) |(F#5) (E5)(F#5) |
| F#m A B |F#m C B | F#m A B |F#m   C B |
| D9 | |

N.C.(F#5)

Verse 1   Deep inside the soul of Mother Earth,

                        D9   E9
Father Time came with a supersonic, supersonic burst.

        N.C.(F#5)
His soul monkey sperm tribes racing to be first up her ruby fruit jungle,

        D9   E9
Givin' bush baby, bush baby birth.

        N.C.(F#5)
The baby was a boy but I think what stunned her

                        D9   E9
Is that this bare breasted baby was a   baby boy, boy, boy, boy wonder.

N.C.(F#5)
Crackin' from his thumb bone came Thelonious Thunder, yeah.

                D9   E9
Fill the sky with hellfire from way down, down, down, down under.

© 1985 MOEBETOBLAME MUSIC and SCREEN GEMS-EMI MUSIC INC.
All Rights Reserved   Used by Permission

	F#m A B F#m A B
Chorus 1	I am a jungle man. I am a jungle man.

F#m   A   B   F#m A   B   F#m
I am a jungle man.   I get all the bush I can.

      A   B   F#m   A   B   F#m
I am a jungle man.   I am a jungle man.

      A   B   F#m   A   B
I am a jungle man.   I get all the bush I

Interlude 1 | N.C.(F#5) (E5) |(F#5)   (E5) (F#5) | (E5) |D9   E9 |
Can.

                 N.C.(F#5)
Verse 2   E-rupting from the ground in Hollywood he glowed.

                                      D9   E9
His jungle turned to concrete, his funk bone, bone, bone, bone to stone.

                 N.C.(F#5)
Like a full blown volcano, I must let it be known

                                  D9   E9
That through this boy's veins atomic lava blood flows and flows.

                 N.C.(F#5)
His soul shocking sounds, they make the mountains moan.

This boy's become a man.

             D9   E9
It's time to   take, take, take, take it to the throne.

                 F#m   A   B   F#m   A   B
Chorus 2   I am a jungle man.   I am a jungle man.

F#m   A   B   F#m A   B
I am a jungle man.   I get all the bush I...

F#m   A   B   F#m   A   B
I am a jungle man.   I am a jungle man.

F#m   A   B   F#m A   B
I am a jungle man.   I get all the bush I...

Interlude 2 ‖: A9 | | | :‖

Guitar Solo ‖: N.C.(F#5) (E5) |(F#5) (E5) (F#5) | (E5) |A* B* :‖

Interlude 3 | N.C.(F#5) (E5) |(F#5) (E5) (F#5) | (E5) |(F#5) (E5) (F#5)|
  | F#5 E5 | F#5 E5 F#5 | E5 | F#5 A5 E5 |
  | | | |

Chorus 3

       F#m   A   B   F#m   A   B
       I am a jungle man.   I am a jungle man.

F#m   A   B   F#m   A   B   F#m
   I am a jungle man.   I get all the bush I can.

     A   B   F#m   A   B
I am a jungle man.   I am a jungle man.

F#m   A   B   F#m   A   B   F#m
   I am a jungle man.   I get all the bush I can.

      A   B   F#m   A   B
‖: I am a jungle man.   I am a jungle man. :‖ *Play 4 times*

Outro | F#5 E5 | F#5 A5 E5 | | F#5 |

RED HOT CHILI PEPPERS

Knock Me Down

Words and Music by Anthony Kiedis,
Flea, John Frusciante and Chad Smith

Melody:

Nev-er too soon _ to _____ be through _ be - in'

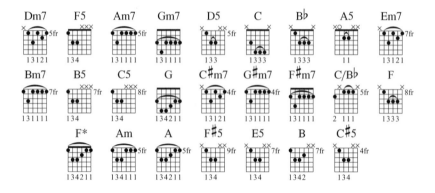

Intro | N.C.(Am7) Dm7 | N.C.(Am7) Dm7 | N.C.(Am7) Dm7 | F5 |

Verse 1

Dm7   Am7 Gm7   D5   C   B♭
    Never too soon   to be through bein' cool, too much ____ too soon.

Dm7   Am7 Gm7   A5   B♭
    Too much for me, too much for you. You're gonna lose in time.

Em7   Bm7 Am7   Em7   D5   C
    Don't be a-fraid to show your friends that you hurt inside, ____ in-side.

Em7   Bm7   Am7
    Pain's part of life, ____ don't hide be-hind your false pride,

    B5   C5
It's a lie, your lie.

© 1989 MOEBETOBLAME MUSIC
All Rights Reserved   Used by Permission

Chorus 1

      D5   C5   D5   C5
If you see me gettin' mighty, if you see me gettin' high,

         Am7   Em7
Knock me down.

   C   G
I'm not bigger than life.

      D5   C5   D5   C5
If you see me gettin' mighty, if you see me gettin' high,

         Am7   Em7
Knock me down.

   C   G
I'm not bigger than life.

Interlude 1

| Dm7   Am7 Gm7 | | Dm7   Am7 B♭ | |

Verse 2

  Dm7   Am7   Gm7   Dm7 C   B♭
  I'm tired of bein' untouch - able, I'm not a-bove   the love.

  Dm7   Am7   Gm7   A5   B♭
  I'm part of you and you're part of me. Why did you go away?

  Em7   Bm7   Am7
  Finding what you're lookin' for

                 C♯m7   G♯m7   F♯m7
Can end up bein',   bein' such a bore.

  Em7   Bm7   Am7
  I pray for you most ev'ry day,

                 C♯m7 G♯m7 F♯m7
My love's with you.   Now fly   a-way.

Chorus 2   *Repeat Chorus 1*

Interlude 2

D5 C/B♭	G	F C B♭	
Am7	F	Am7	F
G	F* Am	A	

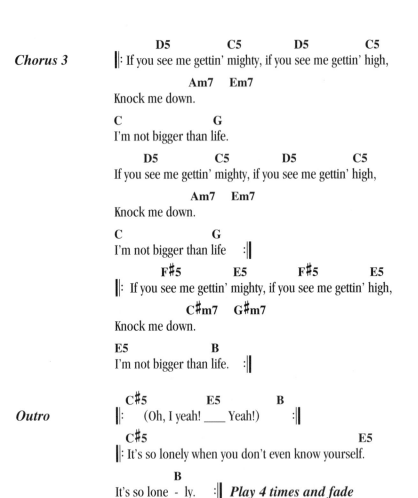

Chorus 3

        D5   C5   D5   C5

‖: If you see me gettin' mighty, if you see me gettin' high,

        Am7   Em7

Knock me down.

C   G

I'm not bigger than life.

     D5   C5   D5   C5

If you see me gettin' mighty, if you see me gettin' high,

        Am7   Em7

Knock me down.

C   G

I'm not bigger than life   :‖

      F#5   E5   F#5   E5

‖: If you see me gettin' mighty, if you see me gettin' high,

        C#m7   G#m7

Knock me down.

E5   B

I'm not bigger than life.   :‖

Outro

    C#5   E5   B

‖:   (Oh, I yeah! ___ Yeah!)   :‖

    C#5   E5

‖: It's so lonely when you don't even know yourself.

         B

It's so lone - ly.   :‖ *Play 4 times and fade*

Love Rollercoaster

Words and Music by Ralph Middlebrooks,
James Williams, Marshall Jones, Leroy Bonner,
Clarence Satchell, Willie Beck and Marvin R. Pierce

Melody:

(Roll - er - coast - er   of love.) ____

C   Bb   A

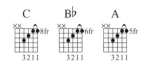

Intro   N.C.
                 You give me that funny feeling in my tummy.

| C   Bb   A | Bb   C |
| Bb   A | Bb   C |
                                Uh-huh.

| Bb   A | Bb   C |
                             Ah,

| Bb   A | Bb   C |
  shit!   Yeah, that's right! Uh-huh.

Pre-Chorus 1
                 C   Bb A   Bb   C
                 (Roller-coaster   of love.) Say what?

                      Bb A   Bb C
                 (Rollercoaster.)   Yeah. (Hoo, hoo, hoo, hoo.)

                      Bb   A   Bb C
                 (Rollercoaster.) Oh, baby, you know what I'm talkin' about.

                      Bb A   Bb C
                 (Rollercoaster.   Hoo, hoo, hoo, hoo.

                      Bb A   Bb   C
                 Rollercoaster.)   Love roller - coaster child.

                      Bb   A   Bb   C
                 (Rollercoaster.) Lovin' you is really __ wild.

                      Bb   A   Bb   C
                 (Rollercoaster.)   Oh, it's __ just a love roll - ercoast - er.

                      Bb A   Bb C
                 (Rollercoaster.)   Step right up and get your ticket.

Copyright © 1976 by Rick's Music Inc.
Copyright Renewed
All Rights Administered by Rightsong Music, Inc.
International Copyright Secured   All Rights Reserved

Chorus 1

N.C.(G5)
(Your love is like a rollercoaster, baby, baby. I wanna ride.

Your love is like a rollercoaster, baby, baby. I wanna ride. Bitch.)

Verse 1

C   Bb   A
Move over, dad, 'cause I'm ___ a double dipper.

Bb   C
Upside down on the zip-zip-zipper.

Bb A   Bb C
One, two, one, two, three. Oh, I got a ticket, so ride with me.

Bb   A   Bb C
Let me go down on the merry-go-round. All is fair on these fair grounds.

Bb A   Bb   C
Let's go slow, let's go fast. Licorice whip gonna whip your ass.

Pre-Chorus 2

C Bb A Bb   C
(Roller-coaster of love.) Say what?

Bb A   Bb C
(Rollercoaster.) Oh, yeah, it's a love roll-ercoast - er.

Bb A   Bb C
(Rollercoaster.) Yeah, go.

Bb A   Bb C
(Rollercoaster.) Can ya get back my love roller-coaster?

Chorus 2 *Repeat Chorus 1*

Verse 2
N.C.(G5)
Move over, dad, 'cause I'm a double dipper.

Upside down on the zip-zip-zipper.

One, two, one, two, three. Well, I got a ticket, so ride with me.

Let me go down on the merry-go-round. All is fair on these fair grounds.

Let's go slow, let's go fast. Licorice whip gonna whip your ass.

Chorus 3

C   B♭ A   B♭   C
(Roller-coaster   of love.) Say what?

          B♭ A   B♭ C
(Rollercoaster.)   Yeah. (Hoo, hoo, hoo, hoo.)

          B♭ A   B♭   C
(Rollercoaster.) Love rollercoaster, ___ child.

          B♭   A   B♭   C
(Rollercoaster.) Lovin' you is all a really ___ wild.

          B♭   A
(Rollercoaster.) Love, love, love, love,

    B♭   C
Love, love, love, love, love, love, love.

          B♭   A   B♭ C
(Rollercoaster.)   Uh-huh. (Hoo, hoo, hoo, hoo.)

Outro
N.C.(G5)
‖:   (Your love is like a rollercoaster,

Baby, baby. I wanna ride.) :‖ ***Repeat and fade***

Me and My Friends

Words and Music by
Anthony Kiedis, Flea,
Hillel Slovak and
Jack Irons

Me and my,me and my,me and my,me and my,me and my   friends. _

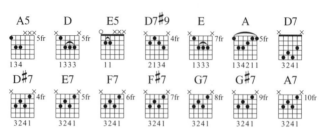

Chorus 1

A5   D
Me and my, me and my, me and my, me and my, me and my friends.
A5   D
Me and my, me and my, me and my, me and my, me and my friends.
A5   D
Me and my, me and my, me and my, me and my, me and my friends.
A5   D
Me and my, me and my, me and my, me and my, me and my friends.

Verse 1

       E5   D7#9   E5   D7#9
Like two sweet peas in an even sweet-er pod,

     E5   D7#9   E5   D7#9
That's __ my friend an' my friend's name is Bob,

       E5   D7#9   E5   D7#9
Like the devil knows hell, I know __ Bob-by well.

     E5   D7#9   E5   D7#9
A well enough to tell you 'bout he's sixty-sev-en smells,

     E5   D7#9   E5   D7#9
A well enough to tell you he's a hella swell ____ fella.

     E5   D7#9   E5   D7#9
A well enough to tell you that we know each oth-er

            E5   D7#9 E5
Better than we know our-selves.

D7#9 E5   D7#9   E5   D7#9
Like freaks of a feather, we rock to-gether.

  E   D7#9   E   D7#9
I know Bobby well, but I think he knows me better.

© 1987 MOEBETOBLAME MUSIC and SCREEN GEMS-EMI MUSIC INC.
All Rights Reserved   Used by Permission

Chorus 2   *Repeat Chorus 1*

| E5 | D7#9 | E5 | D7#9 |

Verse 2
He's as close to me ___ as a friend can be.

| E5 | D7#9 | E5 | D7#9 |

Well, I'll be standin' by my buddy, he'll be standin' by ___ me.

| E5 | D7#9 | E5 | D7#9 |

A just another half of the two-head-ed freak,

| E5 | D7#9 | E5 | D7#9 |

But I need him like ___ my heart needs a beat.

| E5 | D7#9 | E5 | D7#9 |

At this point in this friendly verse,

| E5 | D7#9 | E5 | D7#9 |

I've got to sing a little something that I haven't re-hearsed.

| E5 | D7#9 | E5 | D7#9 |

It's a-bout my man ___ and his name is Hil-lel,

| E5 | D7#9 | E5 | D7#9 |

For who my love is soul broth-er sacred.

| E5 | D7#9 | E5 | D7#9 |

Take it hickle-berry slim boy, ___ take it!

Guitar Solo 1   ‖: E5 D7#9 E5 D7#9 | E5 D7#9 E5 D7#9 :‖ *Play 4 times*

Chorus 3
E   A
Me and my, me and my, me and my, me and my, me and my friends.
E   A
Me and my, me and my, me and my, me and my, me and my friends.

Guitar Solo 2   ‖: N.C.(Dm7) | | | :‖

| E5 | D7#9 | E5 | D7#9 |

Verse 3
Jacky's eyes are closed ___ but he's right on course

| E5 | D7#9 | E5 | D7#9 |

Because he's guided by ___ the in-visible force.

| E5 | D7#9 | E5 | D7#9 |

He drives a kooky green Chrysler, bad as anybod-y's Porsche.

| E5 | D7#9 | E5 | D7#9 |

He's a working class drummer, he's as strong as a horse.

Chorus 4   *Repeat Chorus 1*

Outro | A5 | N.C. | D7   D#7 E7 F7 F#7 G7 | G#7 A7 |

My Friends

Words and Music by Anthony Kiedis,
Flea, Chad Smith and David Navarro

Melody:

My friends are so de-pressed.   I feel the

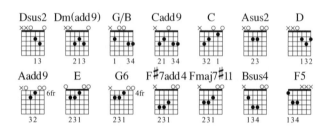

Dsus2 Dm(add9) G/B Cadd9 C Asus2 D
Aadd9 E G6 F#7add4 Fmaj7#11 Bsus4 F5

Intro

‖: Dsus2   Dm(add9) | G/B   Cadd9   :‖

Verse 1

Dsus2   Dm(add9)
   My friends are so depressed.

G/B Cadd9 Dsus2   Dm(add9)
   I feel the question of your loneliness.

G/B   Cadd9   Dsus2   Dm(add9)
   Con-fide 'cause I'll be on your side.

G/B Cadd9   Dsus2   Dm(add9) G/B   Cadd9
   You know I will, ___ you know I will.

Verse 2

Dsus2   Dm(add9)
   Ex-girlfriend called me up,

G/B Cadd9 Dsus2   Dm(add9)
   A-lone and desp'rate on a prison phone.

G/B   Cadd9 Dsus2   Dm(add9) G/B Cadd9
   They want to give her seven years   for being sad.

© 1995 THREE POUNDS OF LOVE MUSIC
All Rights Reserved   Used by Permission

Chorus 1

C   Asus2 C   D   Aadd9
I love all of you   hurt by the cold.

C   Asus2   C   D   Aadd9
So hard and lonely, too,   when you don't know yourself.

Verse 3

Dsus2   Dm(add9)
My friends are so distressed.

G/B   Cadd9 Dsus2   Dm(add9)
They're standing on the brink of emptiness.

G/B   Cadd9 Dsus2   Dm(add9) G/B Cadd9
No words, I know what to ex-press,   this emptiness.

Chorus 2   *Repeat Chorus 1*

Guitar Solo   ‖:D   Dm(add9) |G/B   Cadd9   :‖ *Play 3 times*
               | D   Dm(add9) |G/B   Dm(add9) |

Bridge

E   G6 F♯7add4   Fmaj7♯11
Imagine me ___ taught by tragedy.

    C   Bsus4 F5
Re-lease is peace.

Verse 4

Dsus2   Dm(add9)
I heard a little girl

G/B Cadd9 Dsus2   Dm(add9)
And what she said was something beautiful.

G/B Cadd9 Dsus2   Dm(add9) G/B Cadd9
To give your love no matter what   is what she said.

Chorus 3   *Repeat Chorus 1*

Outro   ‖: D Dm(add9) |G/B   Cadd9 |D Dm(add9) |G/B   Cadd9 :‖
         | Dsus2

One Hot Minute

Words and Music by Anthony Kiedis,
Flea, Chad Smith and David Navarro

Well, I was rid - ing,   rid-ing on my bike. _

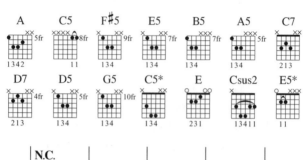

Intro | N.C. | | | | |

Verse 1
N.C.(E7)
Well, I was riding, riding on my bike.

Me with my friend, we're so alike.

(C)   A   C5
Am I all alone?

Verse 2
N.C.(E7)
She said all we a have is this.

We just had to stop and share a kiss.

(C)   A   C5
Am I all alone?

Verse 3
N.C.(E7)
One hot minute and I'm in it, come and get it.

One hot minute and I'm in it, come and get it.

One hot minute and I'm in it, come and get it.

If I chase it I might waste it, come and spin it.

(C)   A N.C.(C)   A
Am I all alone?   Am I all alone?

© 1995 THREE POUNDS OF LOVE MUSIC
All Rights Reserved   Used by Permission

GUITAR CHORD SONGBOOK

Chorus 1

F#5   E5   B5   A5
Sitting in the fire,   a get along and have some fun.

F#5   E5   B5   A5
Floating to be higher,   a maybe I'm your special one.

F#5   E5   B5   A5
Silent testi-fier,   a breathe the moon and eat the sun.

F#5   E5   C7   D7
Sitting in the fire.

Verse 4

N.C.(E7)
   Close your eyes and click your heels.

Can you believe how good it feels?

(C)   A   C5
   Am I all alone?

Verse 5   *Repeat Verse 3*

Chorus 2   *Repeat Chorus 1*

Interlude 1 | E5   D5 G5 D5 | E5   D5 G5 D5 |

Bridge

E5   D5 G5 D5
Say goodbye to where you buy you got it now,

E5   D5 G5 D5
Pay your father, pay your twenty, take a bow.

E5   D5 G5 D5
Say goodbye to where you buy you got it now,

E5   D5 G5 D5
Pay your momma, pay your father, take a bow.

E5   D5 G5 D5
Say goodbye to where you buy you got it now,

E5   D5 G5 D5
Pay your father, pay your twenty, take a bow.

| C7 | D7 C5 |

Interlude 2	| E5	|	|	|	|
	| C5*	| A	| E	|	|
	|	|	| Csus2	| A	|

E
Three pounds of love inside my skull.

A million more lives, it's never dull.

C5*   A
  Just a few times spun,   spun around the sun.

C5*   A
  A couple more or less and __ then we're done.

Chorus 3

F#5   E5 B5   A5
Sitting in the fire,   a get along and have some fun.

F#5   E5   B5   A5
Floating to be higher,   a maybe I'm your special one.

F#5   E5 B5   A5
Silent testi-fier,   a breathe the moon and eat the sun.

F#5   E5
Sitting in the fire.

Outro	||: C7	:|| *Play 15 times*
	| E5*	

Otherside

Words and Music by Anthony Kiedis,
Flea, John Frusciante and Chad Smith

How long, ___ how ___ long _____ will I

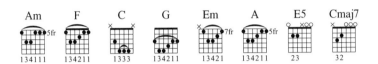

Intro

| Am | F | C | G | |

Chorus 1

Am   F   C
How long, how long will I slide,

G   Am   F
Separate my side?

          C   G   Am   F
I don't, ___ I don't believe it's bad;

C   G
Slit my throat, it's all ___ I ever...

Verse 1

Am   Em
I heard your voice through a photograph;

Am   Em
I thought it up, it brought up the past.

Am   Em
Once you know you can never go back.

         G   A
I've got to take it on the otherside.

© 1999 MOEBETOBLAME MUSIC
All Rights Reserved Used by Permission

Verse 2	Am Em

Verse 2

Am   Em
Centuries are what it meant to me;

Am   Em
A cemetery where I marry the sea.

Am   Em
Stranger things could never change my mind.

              G   A
I've got to take it on the otherside.

G   A
Take it on the otherside.

G   A
Take it on, take it on.

Chorus 2　　　　*Repeat Chorus 1*

Verse 3

Am   Em
Pour my life into a paper cup;

Am   Em
The ashtray's full and I'm spillin' my guts.

Am   Em
She wants to know am I still a slut.

              G   A
I've got to take it on the otherside.

Verse 4

Am   Em
Scarlet starlet and she's in my bed,

Am   Em
A candidate, a, for my soul mate bled.

Am   Em
Push the trigger and pull the thread.

              G   A
I've got to take it on the otherside.

G   A
Take it on the otherside.

G   A
Take it on, take it on.

Chorus 3

Am   F   C
How long, how long will I slide,

G   Am   F
Separate my side?

         C   G   Am   F
I don't, __ I don't believe it's bad;

     C   G
A slittin' my throat, it's all __ I ever...

Bridge

‖: E5 | | Cmaj7 | :‖

E5
Turn me on, take me for a hard ride;

Cmaj7
Burn me out, leave me on the otherside.

E5
I yell and tell it that it's not my friend,

      Cmaj7
I tear it down, I tear it down and then it's born again.

Guitar Solo

| Am | F | C | G |

Chorus 4

Am   F   C
How long, how long will I slide,

G   Am   F
A, separate my side?

         C   G   Am   F
I don't, __ I don't believe it's bad;

     C   G   Am   F
A slittin' my throat, it's all __ I ever had.

         C   G   Am   F
I don't, __ I don't believe it's bad.

     C   G   Am
A, slittin' my throat, it's all __ I ever...

Out in L.A.

Words and Music by
Anthony Kiedis and Flea

Melody:

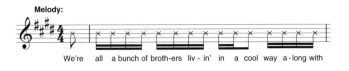

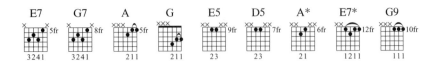

We're all a bunch of broth-ers liv - in' in a cool way a-long with

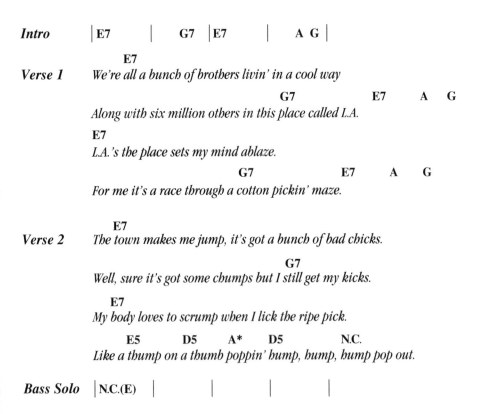

| E7 | G7 | A | G | E5 | D5 | A* | E7* | G9 |

Intro | E7 | G7 | E7 | A G |

Verse 1
                E7
We're all a bunch of brothers livin' in a cool way
                                        G7   E7   A   G
Along with six million others in this place called L.A.
E7
L.A.'s the place sets my mind ablaze.
                            G7   E7   A   G
For me it's a race through a cotton pickin' maze.

Verse 2
                E7
The town makes me jump, it's got a bunch of bad chicks.
                                G7
Well, sure it's got some chumps but I still get my kicks.
            E7
My body loves to scrump when I lick the ripe pick.
            E5   D5   A*   D5   N.C.
Like a thump on a thumb poppin' hump, hump, hump pop out.

Bass Solo | N.C.(E) | | | |

© 1982 MOEBETOBLAME MUSIC
All Rights Reserved   Used by Permission

Verse 3

E7
The action never stops; I'm as wild as can be,

                 G7
Because I'm shooting for the top and my best friend's Flea.

E7
Oom Chucka Willy knew that balls could pop,

     E5   D5   A*   D5   N.C.
But he never met the tree so he never bebopped hop out.

| | | | | |

Verse 4

E7
An-twan the Swan from the pretty fish pond

              G7
Was a bad mother jumper. You could tell he was strong.

   E7
He wore a cold paisley jacket and a hellified ass,

            A   G
And between his legs was a sweet young lass.

   E7
He threw a hundred women up against the wall,

          G7
And he swore to fear that he'd love them all.

     E7
But by the time he got to ninety-nine he had to stop

    E5   D5   A*   D5   E7*
'Cause that's when he thought __ that he heard a fop.

N.C.
Last night and the night before I heard a fop outside

Then I came in doors, rock

| E7 | | G7 | E7 | | G9 |

out.

Verse 5
E7
Now that I told you a little somethin' 'bout the Flea,

Somethin' 'bout the tree, a little somethin' 'bout me,

I can't leave you hangin' 'bout my man Sherm Zee.

         A   G7
He swings the ying, he bangs the yang.

E7
An' now it's time to hear him do his thang.

You better be burnin' Shermin.

Guitar Solo   ‖:E7 | G7 :‖ *Play 3 times*

Outro
E7
We're all a bunch of brothers livin' in a cool way

                     G7
Along with six million others in this place called L.A.

E7   E5   D5 A* D5
            Step out.

Parallel Universe

Words and Music by Anthony Kiedis,
Flea, John Frusciante and Chad Smith

Deep in-side of a par - al - lel

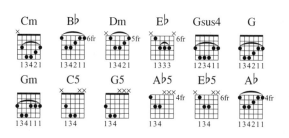

Intro

N.C.			Cm		
Bb			Dm		Eb	
Gsus4		G		

Verse 1

Cm   Bb
Deep inside of a parallel __ universe

Dm   Eb Gsus4 G
It's getting harder and hard - er to tell what came first,

Cm   Bb
Underwater where thoughts can breathe __ easily.

Dm   Eb   Gsus4 Gm   G
Far away you were made __ in a sea, just __ like me.

Chorus 1

C5   G5 Ab5 Eb5
Christ, I'm a side - winder,

   G5
I'm a California king.

C5   G5 Ab5 Eb5
I swear it's __ ev - 'rywhere,

G5
It's ev'rything.

© 1999 MOEBETOBLAME MUSIC
All Rights Reserved Used by Permission

RED HOT CHILI PEPPERS

	Cm	Bb

Verse 2   Staring straight up into the sky, __ oh, my, my.

Dm   **Eb**   **Gsus4**   **G**
A solar system that fits __ in your eye, ___ mi - crocosm.

Cm   **Bb**
You could die but you're never dead, __ spider web.

Dm   **Eb**   **Gsus4**   **Gm**   **G**
Take a look at the stars __ in your head, ___ fields ___ of space, __ kid.

C5   **G5** **Ab5**   **Eb5**

Chorus 2   Christ, I'm a side - winder,

        G5
I'm a   California king.

C5   **G5** **Ab5**   **Eb5**
I swear it's __ ev - 'rywhere,

G5
It's ev'rything.

C5   **G5** **Ab5**   **Eb5**
Christ, I'm a side - winder,

        G5
I'm a   California king.

C5   **G5** **Ab5**   **Eb5**
I swear it's __ ev - 'rywhere,

G5
It's ev'rything.

Interlude　　　| Cm　　　|　　　　|　　　　|　　　　|
　　　　　　　　　|　　　　|　　　　|　　　　|　　　　|

Verse 3

Cm　　　　　　　　　　　　　　　　　　　Bb
　　Psychic changes are born in your heart, __ entertain.

Dm
　　A nervous breakthrough

　　　　　　　　Eb　　　　　Gsus4　　　G
That makes __ us the same, ____ bless __ your heart, girl.

Cm　　　　　　　　　　　　　Bb
　　Kill the pressure it's raining on __ salty cheeks.

Dm　　　　　　　　　　　Eb　　　Gsus4　Gm　　　　G
　　When you hear the belov - ed song, _____ I　　am with __ you.

Chorus 3　　　*Repeat Chorus 2*

Outro　　　‖: Cm　　|　　　| Bb　　　|　　　　|
　　　　　　　　| Dm　　| Ab　　| G　　　|　　　　:‖ *Play 4 times*
　　　　　　　　| Cm

RED HOT CHILI PEPPERS

Porcelain

Words and Music by Anthony Kiedis,
Flea, John Frusciante and Chad Smith

Melody:

Por - c'lain.

Dmaj7   A   F#m   Bm   E

    1 1 1   1 1 1   1 3 4 1 1 1   1 3 4 2 1   2 3 1

Verse 1

    Dmaj7 A   Dmaj7   F#m
    Por - c'lain.   Are you wasting a-way in your skin?

    Dmaj7   A
    Are you missing the love of your kin?

    Dmaj7   F#m
    Drifting and floating and fading away.

    Dmaj7 A   Dmaj7   F#m
    Por - c'lain.   Do you smell like a girl when you smile?

    Dmaj7   A
    Can you bear not to share with your child?

    Dmaj7   F#m
    Drifting and floating and fading away.

Chorus 1

    Bm F#m A
    Lit - tle   lune.

    Bm A
    All day.

    Bm F#m A
    Lit - tle   lune.
    | E | |

© 1999 MOEBETOBLAME MUSIC
All Rights Reserved   Used by Permission

Verse 2

Dmaj7 A   Dmaj7   F♯m
Por - 'clain.   Do you carry the moon in your womb?

Dmaj7   A
Someone said that you're fading too soon.

Dmaj7   F♯m
Drifting and floating and fading away.

Dmaj7 A   Dmaj7   F♯m
Por - 'clain.   Are you wasting a-way in your skin?

Dmaj7   A
Are you missing the love of your kin?

Dmaj7   F♯m
Nodding and melting and fading away.

Chorus 2

Bm F♯m A
Lit - tle   lune.

Bm A
All   day.

Bm F♯m A
Lit - tle   lune.
| E | |

Bm F♯m A
Lit - tle   lune.

Bm A
All   day.

Bm F♯m A
Lit - tle   lune.
| E | | Dmaj7

Purple Stain

Words and Music by Anthony Kiedis,
Flea, John Frusciante and Chad Smith

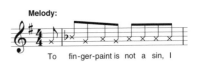

To fin-ger-paint is not a sin, I

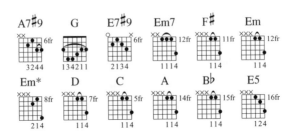

Intro | N.C.(Em) | | |

Verse 1
          N.C.(Em)
To fingerpaint is not a sin, I put my middle finger in.

Your monthly blood is what I win, I'm in your house, now let me spin.

Python, a power, straight from a Monty,

Celluloid loves got a John Frusciante.

Spread your head and spread the blanket,

She's too free and I'm the patient.

Pre-Chorus 1
          A7♯9
A black and white, a red and blue, things that look good on you.

And if I scream, don't let me go; a purple stain, I know.

© 1999 MOEBETOBLAME MUSIC
All Rights Reserved   Used by Permission

GUITAR CHORD SONGBOOK

Verse 2

N.C.(Em)
Knock on wood, we all stay good 'cause we all live in Hollywood

With Dracula and Darla Hood, unspoken words were understood.

Up to my ass in alligators, let's get it on with the alligator haters.

Did what you did, did what you said,

what's the point, yo, what's the spread?

Pre-Chorus 2

A7$\sharp$9
Black and white, a red and blue, things that look good on you.

And if I scream, don't let me go; a purple stain, I know.

And if I call for you to stay come hit the funk on your way.

It's way out there but I don't care 'cause this is where I go.

Chorus 1

G   E7$\sharp$9   G   E7$\sharp$9
Knock on wood, we all stay good 'cause we all live in Hollywood
    G   E7$\sharp$9   G   E7$\sharp$9
With Dracula and Darla Hood, un-spoken words were understood.
G   E7$\sharp$9   G   E7$\sharp$9
Way out there but I don't care 'cause this is what I wanna wear.
G   E7$\sharp$9   G   E7$\sharp$9
Knock on wood, we all stay good 'cause we all live in Hollywood.

Verse 3
N.C.(Em)
To fingerpaint is not a sin, I put my middle finger in.

Your monthly blood is what I win; I'm in your house, now let me spin.

Feather light but you can't a, move this;

Farley is an angel and I can approve this.

Purple is a stain upon my pillow, let's sleep, a weepin' willow.

Pre-Chorus 3   *Repeat Pre-Chorus 2*

Chorus 2   *Repeat Chorus 1*

Interlude | N.C.(E5) | |

Outro

Em7		F#		
Em		F#		
Em*		D		
C		D		
Em		F#	A	
Em		B♭	E5	
Em				
A B♭		E5		

Right on Time

Words and Music by Anthony Kiedis,
Flea, John Frusciante and Chad Smith

One shot, all I need. I've got rhy-thm when I bleed.

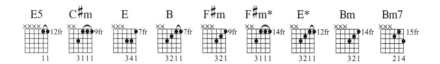

Verse 1

E5
One shot, all I need. I've got rhythm when I bleed.

'Til death do us part. Break my heart so I can start.

Supercalifragilistic, kiss me in the futuristic.

Twisted but I must insist. It's time to get on top of this.

Chorus 1

C#m E   B   F#m C#m E   B   F#m
(It's right on time. It's   right on time.)

C#m   **E**   **B**   **F#m**
It's right on time, it's right on time, it's right on time, it's right on time.

C#m   **E**   **B**   **F#m**
Lookin' fine, you're lookin' fine and get on nineteen-ninety-nine.

© 1999 MOEBETOBLAME MUSIC
All Rights Reserved   Used by Permission

RED HOT CHILI PEPPERS

Verse 2
    E5
Discard to bombard. Calling all you shooting stars.

Holy cow. Bow, wow, wow. Now I'm here, I'm nowhere now.

Joan of Arc reincarnated. Maybe we could be related.

So much blood to circulate, and so much space to decorate.

Chorus 2
C#m E   B F#m C#m E   B F#m
(It's right on time. It's   right on time.)
   C#m   **E**   **B**   **F#m**
It's right on time, it's right on time, it's right on time, it's right on time.
C#m   **E**   **B**   **F#m**
Lookin' fine, you're lookin' fine and get on nineteen-ninety-nine.
 F#m*   **E***   **Bm F#m***   **E* Bm7**
(It's right on time.   It's right on time.
F#m*   **E***   **Bm**   **F#m***   **E* N.C.**
It's right on time.   It's right on time.)

Verse 3
    E5
A plain and simple pain. I want to but I can't complain.

Death row, let us go. It's time to blow up for the show.

All the world reverberated. Coming through we motorcaded.

Vibrate when we operated. Turning up in solid stated.

Outro   ‖: **C#m** | | | :‖
     E5
      Oh, Lord.

Road Trippin'

Words and Music by Anthony Kiedis,
Flea, John Frusciante and Chad Smith

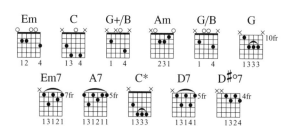

Intro ‖: Em | | C | G+/B :‖

Verse 1

Em   C   G+/B
Road trippin' with my two fav'rite al-lies.

Em   C   G+/B
Fully loaded, we got snacks and supplies.

Em   C   G+/B
It's time to leave this town, it's time to steal away.

Em   C   G+/B
Let's go get lost any-where in the U.S.A.

Em   C   G+/B
Let's go get lost, let's go get lost.

© 1999 MOEBETOBLAME MUSIC
All Rights Reserved   Used by Permission

Chorus 1

Em   C   G+/B
Blue, you sit so pretty west of the one.

Em   C
Sparkles light with yellow icing,

   G+/B   Em
Just a mirror for the sun.

C   G+/B   Em
Just a mirror for the sun.

C   G+/B   Am   G/B   C   G
Just a mirror for the sun.

Am   G/B   C   G
These smiling eyes ___ are just a mirror for...

Verse 2

Em   C   G+/B
So much as came before those battles lost and won.

Em   C   G+/B
This life is shining more for-ever in the sun.

Chorus 2

Em   C   G+/B
Now let us check our heads and let us check the surf.

Em   C   G   Em
Staying high and dry's more trouble than it's worth in the sun.

C   G+/B   Em
Just a mirror for the sun.

C   G+/B   Am   G/B   C   G
Just a mirror for the sun. _____

Am   G/B   C   G
These smiling eyes ___ are just a mirror for…

Interlude

‖: Em7 | A7 | C* | D7 |
| Em7 | A7 | C* | D#7   :‖

Verse 3

Em   C   G+/B
In Big Sur we take some time to linger on.

Em   C   G+/B
We three hunky dories got our snake finger on.

Em   C   G+/B
Now let us drink the stars, it's time to steal away.

Em   C   G+/B
Let's go get lost right here in the U.S.A.

Em   C G+/B
Let's go get lost, let's go get lost.

Chorus 3

Em   C   G+/B
Blue, you sit so pretty west of the one.

Em   C
Sparkles light with yellow icing,

 G+/B   Em
Just a mirror for the sun.

C G+/B   Em
Just a mirror for the sun.

C G+/B   Am G/B C G
Just a mirror for the sun.

Am   G/B   C G
These smiling eyes ___ are just a mirror for…

Am   G/B   C G
These smiling eyes ___ are just a mirror for…

Am   G/B   C G
Your smiling eyes ___ are just a mirror for…

Outro   ‖: Em | | | :‖ *Play 3 times*

Save the Population

Words and Music by Anthony Kiedis,
Flea, John Frusciante and Chad Smith

Melody:

His - to - ry ___ so strong. ___

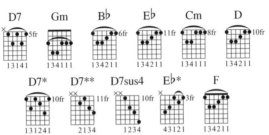

D7   Gm   B♭   E♭   Cm   D

D7*   D7**   D7sus4   E♭*   F

Intro

| N.C.(Gm) (B♭) | (Dm) | (Gm) (B♭) | (Dm7) | |
| (Gm) (B♭) | (Dm) | (Gm) (B♭) | (Dm) | |

Verse 1

N.C.(Gm) (B♭)   (Dm) (Gm) (B♭)   (Dm9)
History _____ so strong.   History _____ so strong.

(Gm) (B♭)   (Dm) (Gm(add4)) (B♭)   (Gm) (D(♭5))
History _____ so strong.   History _____ so strong.

(Gm)   (B♭)   (Dm7)
Sink another drink, it's ___ song the honky tonk will do.

(Gm)   (B♭)   (Dm)
Make another break and ___ bomb your fav'rite ingenue.

(Gm) (B♭)   (D) (Gm)   (B♭)   D7
This the dis - tant dawn.   This the dis - tant dawn.

Pre-Chorus 1

Gm   B♭
I put my cards upon the table.   I do this feat 'cause I am able.

Gm
One picks his broken down devotion.

B♭
I threw my pistol in the ocean.

E♭   Cm
Eyes wide with revelation.   Shine at the police station.

D D7* D   D7*
And when the ver - dict comes 'round,

D7**   D7sus4
I'm sure that you will go down.

© 2003 MOEBETOBLAME MUSIC
All Rights Reserved Used by Permission

Chorus 1

Eb*   F   Gm
Stay all night, we'll save __ the popula - tion.

Eb*   F   Gm
Stay all night, we'll save __ the popula - tion.

Eb*   F   Gm
Stay all night, we'll save __ the popula - tion.

Eb*   F   Gm
Stay all night, we'll save __ the popula - tion.

Interlude

| N.C.(Gm) (Bb) | (Dm) | (Gm) (Bb) | (Dm) |

| (Gm) (Bb) | (Dm) | (Gm(add4)) (Bb) | (D5) (D(B5)) |

Verse 2

N.C.(Gm) (Bb) (Dm) (Gm)
Pistol and _____ it's pawn, _____ sail it

  (Bb) (Dm)
Through the ___ lexicon.

 (Gm) (Bb)
A pistol and ___ it's pawn,

(Dm) (Gm(add4)) (Bb)   (D5) (D(b5))
  Blood and border ___ lines be drawn.

(Gm)   (Bb)   (Dm7)
Take another bottle ___ down that brought the lamb, the shrew.

(Gm)   (Bb)   (Dm)
Make another offer, ___ sound the ride, the gothic through.

(Gm) (Bb) (D) (Gm) (Bb) D7
History ___ so strong. History ___ so strong.

Pre-Chorus 2 *Repeat Pre-Chorus 1*

Chorus 2

Eb*   F   Gm
‖: Stay all night we'll save ___ the popula - tion.

(Stay all night we'll save the population.) :‖ ***Play 6 times***

Scar Tissue

Words and Music by Anthony Kiedis,
Flea, John Frusciante and Chad Smith

Melody:

Scar tis-sue that I wish you saw, __

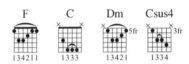

F   C   Dm   Csus4

134211   1333   13421   1334

Intro | F   C | Dm   C | F   C | Dm |

Verse 1
    F   C Dm   C
    Scar tissue that I wish you saw, ___ sarcastic mister know it all.

    F   C Dm
    Close your eyes and I'll kiss you 'cause ___ with the birds I'll share,

Chorus 1
    F   C Dm   C
    With the birds I'll share this lone   -   ly view,

    F   C Dm   C
    With the birds I'll share this lone   -   ly view.

Verse 2
    F   C Dm   C
    Push me up against the wall, ___ young Kentucky girl in a push up bra.

    F   C Dm   C
    Fallin' all over myself to lick   your heart and taste your health 'cause

© 1999 MOEBETOBLAME MUSIC
All Rights Reserved   Used by Permission

Chorus 2

    F   C Dm   C
With the birds I'll share this lone -   ly view,

    F   C Dm   C
With the birds I'll share this lone -   ly view.

    F   Csus4   C Dm
With the birds I'll share this lone -   ly view.

Interlude | Dm | | C | Dm |

Verse 3

    F   C
Blood loss in a bathroom stall,

Dm   C
Southern girl with a scarlet drawl.

    F   C   Dm
Wave goodbye to ma and pa 'cause ____ with the birds I'll share,

Chorus 3   *Repeat Chorus 1*

Verse 4

    F   C Dm   C
Soft spoken with a broken jaw, ____ step outside, but not to brawl.

    F
Autumn's sweet, we call it fall,

C Dm
I'll make it to the moon if I have to crawl.

Chorus 4   *Repeat Chorus 2*

Guitar Solo | Dm | | C | Dm |
                  | | | C | Dm |

Verse 5   *Repeat Verse 1*

Chorus 5   *Repeat Chorus 2*

Outro ||:Dm | | C | Dm   :|| *Play 4 times*

Soul to Squeeze

from the Paramount Motion Picture
THE CONEHEADS

Words and Music by Anthony Kiedis,
Flea, John Frusciante and Chad Smith

Melody:

I got a bad dis-ease, ___

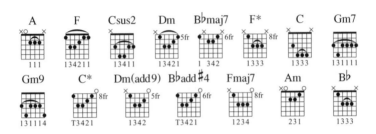

Intro

‖: A | | | :‖

‖: F Csus2 | Dm B♭maj7 | Dm F* C | Gm7 Gm9 :‖

Verse 1

N.C.(F)　(C)　　　(Dm) (B♭) (Dm)　　　(F)　(C)　(Gm)
　　I got a bad disease,　　　　all from my brain is where I bleed.

(F)　(C)　　　(Dm) (B♭) (Dm)　　　(F)　(C)　(B♭)
　Insani-ty, it seems,　　　　has got me by my soul to squeeze.

F　　　Csus2　　Dm　B♭maj7
　Well, all the love for me,

Dm　　　F*　C　Gm7 Gm9
　With all the dying trees I scream.

F　　　Csus2　　Dm　B♭maj7
　The angels in my dreams,　　yeah,

Dm　　　F*　　C　　Gm7 Gm9
　Have turned to demons of greed, that's me.

Copyright © 1991 by Ensign Music Corporation and Moebetoblame Music
International Copyright Secured All Rights Reserved

Chorus 1

F*   C*   Dm(add9)   B♭add♯4
Where I go I just don't know.   I got to, got to, gotta take it slow.

Fmaj7   C*
When I've found my piece of mind

Dm(add9)   Am   B♭
I'm gonna give you some of my good time.

Verse 2

N.C.(F)   (C)   (Dm) (B♭)
Today love smiled on me,

(Dm)   (F)   (C)   (Gm)
It took a-way my pain, say please.

(F)   (C)   (Dm) (B♭) (Dm)   (F) (C)   (B♭)
Oh, let your ride be free,   you gotta let it be, oh yeah.

Chorus 2   *Repeat Chorus 1*

Guitar Solo

| N.C.(F) (C) | (Dm) (B♭) | (Dm) (F)(C) | (Gm) | |
| (F)   (C) | (Dm) (B♭) | (Dm) (F)(C) | | |

Interlude

| Dm C | Am | Dm C | Am | |
| Dm C | Am | Dm C | Am B♭ | |

Verse 3

N.C.(F)   (C)   (Dm) (B♭) (Dm)   (F) (C)   (Gm)
Oh, so po-lite indeed,   well, I got ev'ry-thing I need.

(F)   (C)   (Dm) (B♭)
Oh, make my days agree

(Dm)   (F)   (C)   (B♭)
And take a-way my self-de-struction.

F   C
It's bitter, baby, and it's very sweet.

  Dm   B♭maj7
Ho - ly roller coaster but I'm on my feet.

Dm   F*
Take me to the river, let me on your shore,

    C   Gm7
Well, I'll be comin' back, baby, I'll be comin' back for more.

F   Csus2   Dm
Do, do, do, do, ding, a, zing, ___ a, dong, dong, ga, ding,

                B♭maj7
Ba, da, ma, sa, ma, na, ma, cong, gong, yeah.

Dm   F*   C
I could not forget, but I __ would not endeavor simple pleasures.

          Gm7   Gm9
I'm much better, but I won't re-gret it never.

Chorus 3

Fmaj7   C*   Dm(add9)   B♭add♯4
Where I go I just don't know.   I got to, got to, gotta take it slow.

Fmaj7   C*
When I've found my piece of mind

Dm(add9)   Am   B♭
I'm gonna give you some of my good time.

Fmaj7   C*
Where I go I just don't know.

Dm(add9)   B♭add♯4
I might end up somewhere in Mexico.

Fmaj7   C*
When I've found my piece of mind

Dm(add9)   Am B♭   F
I'm gonna keep it for the end of time.

Special Secret Song Inside

Words and Music by Anthony Kiedis,
Flea, Hillel Slovak and Jack Irons

Melody:

Well, my la - la-dy, she lives

Dm7   Em7   Dm   C   F   Em

Intro	|Dm7 | | | |

Verse 1
Dm7
Well, my lady, she lives three houses away,

And she claims that she can hear moaning and screaming

To me fuckin' you every night. Well, let me lay.

Chorus 1
Dm7
I want to party on your pussy, baby.

Well, I want to party, party on your pussy.

I want to party on your pussy, baby.

Well, I want to party on your pussy. Yeah, yeah, yeah.

Interlude   \|Dm7 \| \| \| \|

© 1987 MOEBETOBLAME MUSIC and SCREEN GEMS-EMI MUSIC INC.
All Rights Reserved   Used by Permission

	Dm7
Verse 2	Struck by lust in a telephone booth,

Busted by a cop, he said, "That's uncool."

Well, he said that he hears moaning and screaming

To me fuckin' you every night. Well, let me say, "Hey."

Chorus 2   *Repeat Chorus 1*

	N.C.
Breakdown	I want to party on your pussy, baby.

I want to party on your pussy.

I want to party on your pussy, baby.

I want to party on your pussy.

	Em7
Chorus 3	Well, I want to party on your pussy, baby.

Well, I want to party on your pussy.

I want to party on your pussy, baby.

I want to party on your pussy.

I want to party all over your pussy, girl.

I want to party on your pussy.

Bridge

N.C.(Am)
Let me shine your diamond;

The girl got a scratch.

Slap that cat.

Have mercy.

Guitar Solo

| Dm | C | Dm | C | |
| F | Em | | | |

Outro

Dm7
I want to party on your pussy, baby.

Well, I want to party, party on your pussy.

Well, I want to party on your pussy, baby.

I want to party on your pussy.

Subway to Venus

Words and Music by Anthony Kiedis,
Flea, John Frusciante and Chad Smith

Melody:

Step right up   and lis-ten please, _

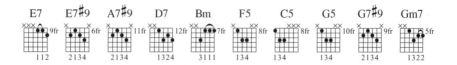

E7   E7♯9   A7♯9   D7   Bm   F5   C5   G5   G7♯9   Gm7

Intro |E7 | | | |
              |E7♯9 | | | |

                        E7♯9
Verse 1   *Step right up and listen please,*

                You're gonna get it with the greatest of ease.

                Well, well, ev'rybody, uh, gather 'round, all aboard the underground.

                You've got to get in before you get out,

                And gettin' out is what it's gonna be about.

                Well, if you find that you are blind, open up your bashful mind.
                A7♯9
                Let my band step inside, take you on a cosmic ride.
                            D7   E7♯9
                I let my band step inside, take you on a cosmic ride.

© 1989 MOEBETOBLAME MUSIC
All Rights Reserved   Used by Permission

Verse 2

E7$\sharp$9

With honest sounds, I'll paint your brain. For in this song, I do proclaim

That once aboard this moving train, I'll do my best to ease your pain.

Slinky as my speech may be, on this trip, you'll ride for free.

And as we leave our trail of spots, well, outer space is not so dark.

A7$\sharp$9

This axis bold as love you see, comes and goes so easily.

D7   E7$\sharp$9

This axis bold as love you see, comes and goes so easily.

Chorus 1

Bm   F5 C5   G5

Space is king, or so I sing, a subway to Ve - nus.

Bm   F5 C5   G5

Space is king, or so I sing, a subway to Ve - nus.

| E7$\sharp$9 | | | |

Verse 3

E7$\sharp$9

Once aboard and feeling smooth, like a liquid you will ooze.

Into a state of mind that soothes, aw, be my guest inside my groove.

'Cause what I've got to give you is gonna make you wanna boogalulu.

I'll make you wiggle like a wiggly worm

'Cause you deserve to wiggle and squirm.

A7$\sharp$9

Life's too short to be in a hole, so bust into your funkiest stroll.

D7   E7$\sharp$9

Life's too short to be in a hole, so bust into your funkiest stroll.

Chorus 2   *Repeat Chorus 1*

Interlude

```
| G7#9    |          |          |          |
| E7#9    |          |          |          |
| Gm7     | N.C.     |          |          |
```

        E7#9

Verse 4   *What I got to give to you is gonna make you wanna boogalulu.*

    I'll make you wiggle like a wiggly worm

    'Cause you deserve to wiggle and squirm.

    Life's too short to be in a hole, so bust into your funkiest stroll.

    Well, take your body, uh, shake it around and do the dog on the ground.

    And if I can't make you dance,

    I guess I'll just have to make you piss your pants.

    Bm   F5 C5   G5

Chorus 3   Space is king, or so I sing, a subway to Ve - nus.

    Bm   F5 C5   G5

    Space is king, or so I sing, subway to Ve - nus.

    Bm   F5 C5   G5

    Space is king, or so I sing, subway to Ve - nus.

    Bm   F5 C5   G5

    Space is king, o, o, o, or so I sing, subway to Ve - nus.

Outro

```
| E7            |          |          |          |
||: E7#9        |          |          |  :|| Play 3 times
| F5  C5  G5    |
```

Suck My Kiss

Words and Music by Anthony Kiedis,
Flea, John Frusciante and Chad Smith

Melody:

Well, I'm sail-in'.   Yeah! _

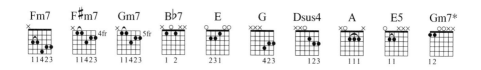

Fm7 F#m7 Gm7 Bb7 E G Dsus4 A E5 Gm7*

Intro

N.C.(Gm7)
Well, I'm sailin'. Yeah! Yeah! Oh, yeah!

Yeah! Yeah! Oh, yeah! Hit me!

Verse 1

N.C.(Gm7)
Should have been, could have been, would have been dead

If I didn't get the message goin' to my head.

I am what I am, most motherfuckers don't give a damn.

Fm7   **F#m7**
  Oh, baby, think you can? Be my girl, I'll be your man.

Gm7   **N.C.(Gm7)**
Someone full of fun, do me till I'm well done.

Little Bo Peep cumin' from my stun gun.

Beware, take care, most motherfuckers have a cold-ass stare.

Fm7   **F#m7**   **Gm7 Bb7**
  Oh, baby, please be there, suck my kiss, cut me my share.

© 1991 MOEBETOBLAME MUSIC
All Rights Reserved   Used by Permission

RED HOT CHILI PEPPERS

Chorus 1

    E   G Dsus4   G   Dsus4 A
Hit me! You _____ can't ___ hurt me!   Suck my kiss!

    E   G   Dsus4 G   Dsus4 A
Kiss me! Please _____ per - vert me!   Stick with this!

        G Dsus4 G   Dsus4 A E5
Is she talk - ing ___ dirt-y?

    E   G Dsus4 G
Give to me sweet sa - cred ___ bliss,

Dsus4 A
Your mouth was made to suck my kiss!

Verse 2

N.C.(Gm7)
Look at me, can't you see, all I really want to be

Is free from a world that hurts me.

I need relief, do you want me girl to be your thief?

Fm7   **F#m7**
Oh, baby, just for you I'd steal anything that you want me to.

Gm7 N.C.(Gm7)
K-i-s-s-i-n-g, chicka chickadee, do me like a banshee.

Lowbrow, is how, swimming in the sound of bow wow wow.

Fm7   **F#m7**   **Gm7** **Bb7**
Oh, baby, do me now, do me here I do allow.

Chorus 2

```
E        G  Dsus4      G       Dsus4  A
  Hit me! You _____ can't ___ hurt me!        Suck my kiss!

E        G      Dsus4  G    Dsus4  A
  Kiss me! Please _____ per - vert me!        Stick with this!

     G  Dsus4  G        Dsus4  A   E5
Is she gon  -  na __ curt-sy?

E                 G  Dsus4  G        Dsus4 A
Give to me sweet sa  -  cred __ bliss, that    mouth was made to.
```

Guitar Solo

```
‖: Gm7*  |          |          |        :‖
```

Verse 3   *Repeat Verse 1*

Chorus 3

```
E        G  Dsus4      G       Dsus4  A
  Hit me! You _____ can't ___ hurt me!        Suck my kiss!

E        G      Dsus4  G    Dsus4  A
  Kiss me! Please _____ per - vert me!        Stick with this!

     G  Dsus4  G        Dsus4  A   E5
Is she talk  -  ing __ dirt-y?

E                 G  Dsus4  G
Give to me sweet sa  -  cred __ bliss,

Dsus4  A
Your   mouth was made to suck my kiss!
```

Taste the Pain

Words and Music by Anthony Kiedis,
Flea, John Frusciante and Darren Henley

Melody:

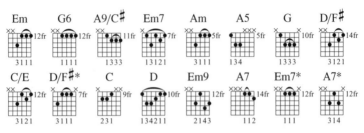

Flat   on my back   in a   lone-ly   sprawl, __

Em   G6   A9/C♯   Em7   Am   A5   G   D/F♯
C/E   D/F♯*   C   D   Em9   A7   Em7*   A7*

Intro | N.C. | | | |

Verse 1
        Em   G6   A9/C♯
Flat on my back in a lonely sprawl,

          Em   G6   A9/C♯   Em   G6
I stare at the ceil - ing 'cause I cannot fall a-sleep tonight,

A9/C♯ Em   G6 A9/C♯
   A no a not at all.

        Em   G6   A9/C♯
Headlights flash across my bedroom wall,

          Em   G6   A9/C♯   Em   G6
A crying eyes open 'cause I cannot fall in love with you,

A9/C♯ Em   G6 A9/C♯
   A no not at all.

Chorus 1
        Em7   Am   G6
Walk away an' taste the pain,   come again some other day.

        Em7   Am   G6
Aren't you glad you weren't afraid,   funny how the price gets paid.

Em7   Am   G6
   Walk away an' taste the pain,   come again some other day.

Em7
   Well, aren't you glad you were not afraid,

Am   G6   Em G6 A9/C♯
   Funny how the price gets paid.

© 1989 MOEBETOBLAME MUSIC and FOX FILM MUSIC CORPORATION
All Rights Reserved   Used by Permission

Verse 2

```
Em       G6        A9/C♯      Em       G6
Busted in two a like a brittle stick, I cannot drink
            A9/C♯                Em       G6
Because my throat constricts a love sick from you,
A9/C♯          Em      G6 A9/C♯
A that would never do.
Em       G6            A9/C♯
Open my mouth I couldn't make a sound.
  Em              G6            A9/C♯
I could not scream, ___ you know I cannot shout.
   Em       G6 A9/C♯  Em   G6 A9/C♯
It's up to you,      a noth-ing to do.
```

Chorus 2

```
Em7                          Am            G6
Walk away an' taste the pain,    come again some other day.
Em7                              Am            G6
Aren't you glad you weren't afraid,    funny how the price gets paid.
Em7                          Am            G6
Walk away an' taste the pain,    come again some other day.
Em7
Well, aren't you glad you were not afraid,
Am           G6          A5  G
Funny how the price gets paid.
   D/F♯   C/E   A5   G     D/F♯*   C    D
Ah.        Yeah, ___    yeah!
```

Interlude

```
‖: Em  G6  │ A9/C♯     │ Em  G6  │ A9/C♯     :‖
│ Em9 N.C. │           │ Em9 N.C. │            │
```

Verse 3

Em G6 A9/C♯
This may come as a shocking surprise,

 Em   G6   A9/C♯
I have to take a walk I have to kiss it goodbye.

  Em G6 A9/C♯
Good-bye my love.

   Em   G6 A9/C♯ Em G6 A9/C♯
A good-bye my love. _____ I am not alive.

Chorus 3

Em7   Am   G6
 Walk away an' taste the pain, come again some other day.

Em7   Am   G6
 Aren't you glad you weren't afraid, funny how the price gets paid.

Em7   Am   G6
 Walk away an' taste the pain, come again some other day.

Em7
 Well, aren't you glad you were not afraid,

Am   G6 Em7 Am
 Funny how the price gets paid,

   G6   Em7
How the price gets paid.

Am   G6 Em7 Am   G6   Em7
Well. I, I, I, I, I, I, I a, well, I got to pay the price.

Am   G6   Em7
 I think I'll walk away.

Am G6   Em7
Ev'ryday it's okay if you want to play it again.

Am   G6
 I got to pay the price.

Outro

‖: Em | A7 | Em | A7 |

| Em7* | A7* | Em9 | A7   :‖ *Repeat and fade*

Tearjerker

Words and Music by Anthony Kiedis,
Flea, Chad Smith and David Navarro

Melody:

My mouth fell o - pen ___ hop-in' that the truth ___

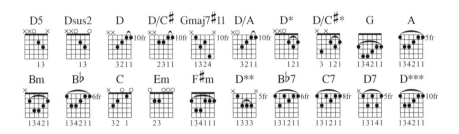

D5   Dsus2   D   D/C♯   Gmaj7♯11   D/A   D*   D/C♯*   G   A

Bm   B♭   C   Em   F♯m   D**   B♭7   C7   D7   D***

Intro

D5	Dsus2			

Spoken: "Could you turn up the track a little bit, please?"

‖: D   D/C♯ | Gmaj7♯11   D/A |
| D   D/C♯ | Gmaj7♯11   :‖

Verse 1

D*   D/C♯*   G   A   D*
My mouth fell o - pen   hopin' that the truth ___ would not be true.

D/C♯*   Bm   D*   D/C♯*
Re-fuse the news.   I'm feelin' sick now.

G   A   D*
What the fuck am I ___ supposed to do, ___ just

D/C♯*   Bm   A   B♭   A   B♭   A
Lose and lose.

© 1995 THREE POUNDS OF LOVE MUSIC
All Rights Reserved   Used by Permission

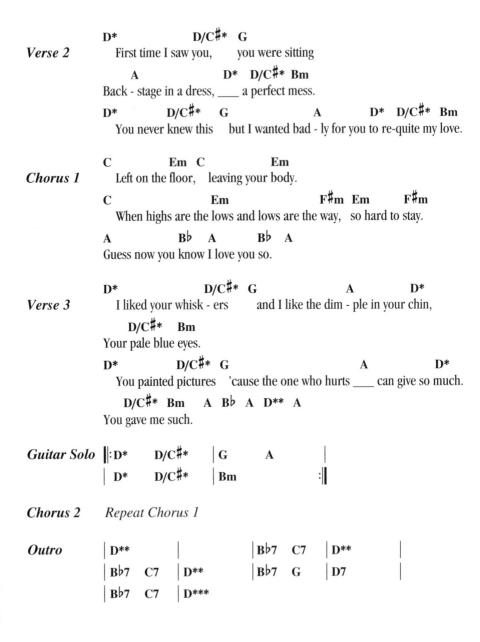

Verse 2

D*   D/C#* G
First time I saw you,   you were sitting

      A   D* D/C#* Bm
Back - stage in a dress, ___ a perfect mess.

D*   D/C#*   G   A   D* D/C#* Bm
You never knew this   but I wanted bad - ly for you to re-quite my love.

Chorus 1

C   Em C   Em
Left on the floor,   leaving your body.

C   Em   F#m Em   F#m
When highs are the lows and lows are the way,   so hard to stay.

A   Bb   A   Bb   A
Guess now you know I love you so.

Verse 3

D*   D/C#* G   A   D*
I liked your whisk - ers   and I like the dim - ple in your chin,

    D/C#* Bm
Your pale blue eyes.

D*   D/C#* G   A   D*
You painted pictures 'cause the one who hurts ___ can give so much.

    D/C#* Bm   A Bb A D** A
You gave me such.

Guitar Solo ‖:D*   D/C#* |G   A |
                | D*   D/C#* |Bm   :‖

Chorus 2   *Repeat Chorus 1*

Outro | D** | |Bb7 C7 |D** |
          | Bb7 C7 |D** |Bb7 G |D7 |
          | Bb7 C7 |D***

Throw Away Your Television

Words and Music by Anthony Kiedis,
Flea, John Frusciante and Chad Smith

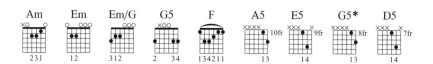

Throw a - way _ your   tel - e - vi - sion.

| Am | Em | Em/G | G5 | F | A5 | E5 | G5* | D5 |

Intro

‖: N.C.(A5) | (E5) | (A5) | (E5) :‖

Verse 1

N.C. (A5)   (E5)   (A5)   (E5)
Throw away your television. Time to make this clean decision.

(A5)   (E5)   (A5)
Master waits for it's collision now.

(E5)   (A5) (E5)   (A5)
    It's a repeat   of a story told.

(E5)   (A5) (E5)   (A5)   (E5)
    It's a repeat   and it's getting old.

Verse 2

N.C. (A5)   (E5)   (A5)   (E5)
Throw away your television. Make a break, big intermission.

(A5)   (E5)   (A5)
Recreate your supervision now.

(E5)   (A5) (E5)   (A5)
    It's a repeat   of a story told.

(E5)   (A5) (E5)   (A5)   (E5)
    It's a repeat   and it's getting old.

© 2002 MOEBETOBLAME MUSIC
All Rights Reserved   Used by Permission

Chorus 1

Am   Em   Em/G
Renegades with fancy gaug-es

Am   Em   Em/G
  Slay the plague for it's conta-gious.

Am   Em   Em/G
Pull the plug and take the stag-es.

G5   F   N.C. (A5)
Throw away your television now.

Interlude

| N.C.(A5) | (E5) | (A5) | (E5) | |
              Oy, oy, oy.

Verse 3

N.C.(A5)   (E5)   (A5)   (E5)
Throw away your television. Take the noose off your ambition.

(A5)   (E5)   (A5)
Reinvent your intuition now.

(E5)   (A5) (E5)   (A5)
  It's a repeat   of a story told.

(E5)   (A5) (E5) ·   (A5) (E5)
  It's a repeat   and it's getting old.

Chorus 2   *Repeat Chorus 1*

Guitar Solo   ‖: A5 | E5 | G5* | D5   :‖ *Play 4 times*

Verse 4

Am   Em Em/G Am   Em Em/G
Throw away your televi-sion.   Salivate to repeti-tion.

Am   Em   Em/G Am Em   Em/G   Am
'Levitate this ill condi-tion now,   it's a re-peat.

Em   Em/G Am Em   Em/G Am
  It's a re-peat.   It's a re-peat.

Em   Em/G Am Em   Em/G Am
  It's a re-peat.   It's a re-peat.

True Men Don't Kill Coyotes

Words and Music by Anthony Kiedis,
Flea, Cliff Martinez and Jack Sherman

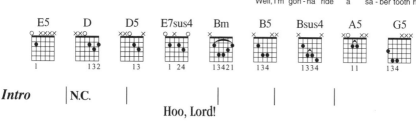

E5	D	D5	E7sus4	Bm	B5	Bsus4	A5	G5
1	132	13	1 24	13421	1 34	1334	11	134

Intro | N.C. | | | | |

Hoo, Lord!

Verse 1
       E5   D   E5   D5
Well, I'm gonna ride a saber tooth horse through the Hollywood Hills.

       E5
The farther west, the farther out,

D   E5   E7sus4   E5   D   E5   D5
Yeah, that's the way I feel.

       E5   D   E5   D5
Well, I dig the dirt an' I dig the dust. I barbecue my meals.

Bm   B5   D5   E5
Ridin' wild on a paisley dragon through the Hollywood Hills, yeah.

       D5   E5   D5
Huh, Hollywood Hills.

Verse 2
       E5   D   E5   D5
Well, I'm gonna ride a saber tooth horse through the Hollywood Hills.

       E5   D5
And just don't show me any-thing

       E5   E7sus4   E5   D5   E5   D5
'Cause that's the way I feel.

       E5   D   E5   D5
Well, I dig the dirt an' I dig the dust. I barbecue my meals.

Bm   B5   D5   E5
Ridin' wild on a paisley dragon through the Hollywood Hills, yeah.

       D5   E5   D5
Huh, Hollywood Hills.

© 1984 MOEBETOBLAME MUSIC and SCREEN GEMS-EMI MUSIC INC.
All Rights Reserved   Used by Permission

Chorus 1

B5
Passion dripping from the coyote's eyes.

                    D
He can taste his blood an' blood never lies.

                        E5   D5   E5 D5   E5
Spoken: Pale face die. True men don't   kill coyotes.

            D5   E5 D5   E5   D5   E5   D5
True men don't   kill coyotes.

Verse 3   *Repeat Verse 1*

Chorus 2

B5
Passion dripping from the coyote's eyes.

                    D
He can taste his blood an' blood never lies.

                        E5   D5   E5   D5
Spoken: Pale face die. True men don't   kill coyotes.

E5   D5
  True men don't.

Interlude 1 | E5   D | Bsus4 | | | |

Verse 4   *Repeat Verse 2*

Chorus 3   *Repeat Chorus 2*

Interlude 2 *Repeat Interlude 1*

Outro

E5   D5   E5   D5   E5   D5
  True men don't   kill coyotes.   True men don't.

| E5   D5 | A5 | | | |
                                                    Ow!

E5   D5   E5   D5   E5   D5   E5   G5
  True men don't   kill coyotes.   True men don't.

Under the Bridge

Words and Music by
Anthony Kiedis, Flea,
John Frusciante and
Chad Smith

Some-times I feel _ like I don't have a part - ner.

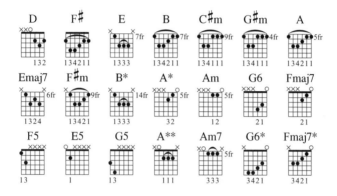

Intro   ‖: **D** |**F#** |**D** |**F#**   :‖

Verse 1

    E   **B**   **C#m**   **G#m A**
Sometimes I feel like I don't have a part - ner.

    E   **B**   **C#m**   **A**
Sometimes I feel like my only friend

       E   **B**   **C#m G#m** **A**
Is the city I live in, the city of an   - gels.

    E   **B**   **C#m**   **A**   **Emaj7**
Lonely as I am, to-gether we cry.

© 1991 MOEBETOBLAME MUSIC
All Rights Reserved   Used by Permission

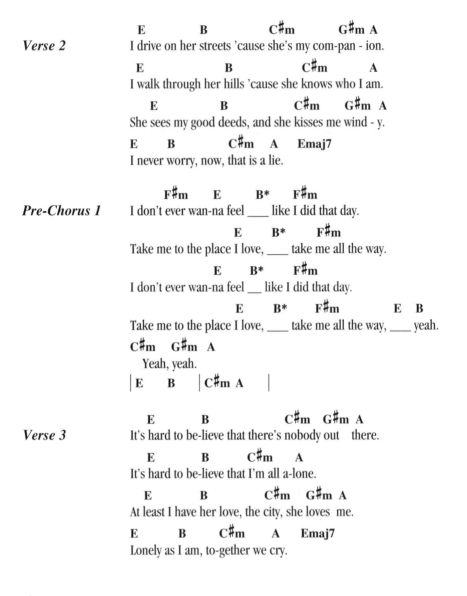

Verse 2

      E   B   C#m   G#m A
I drive on her streets 'cause she's my com-pan - ion.

      E   B   C#m   A
I walk through her hills 'cause she knows who I am.

       E   B   C#m   G#m A
She sees my good deeds, and she kisses me wind - y.

      E   B   C#m   A   Emaj7
I never worry, now, that is a lie.

Pre-Chorus 1

         F#m   E   B*   F#m
I don't ever wan-na feel ____ like I did that day.

            E   B*   F#m
Take me to the place I love, ____ take me all the way.

            E   B*   F#m
I don't ever wan-na feel __ like I did that day.

             E   B*   F#m   E B
Take me to the place I love, ____ take me all the way, ____ yeah.

C#m G#m A
  Yeah, yeah.

| E   B | C#m A |

Verse 3

      E   B   C#m G#m A
It's hard to be-lieve that there's nobody out   there.

      E   B   C#m   A
It's hard to be-lieve that I'm all a-lone.

      E   B   C#m G#m A
At least I have her love, the city, she loves me.

      E   B   C#m   A   Emaj7
Lonely as I am, to-gether we cry.

Pre-Chorus 2

<pre>
       F#m   E   B*   F#m
I don't ever wan-na feel ___ like I did that day.
                       E   B*   F#m
Take me to the place I love, ___ take me all the way.
                 E   B*   F#m
I don't ever wan-na feel ___ like I did that day.
                 E   B*   F#m
Take me to the place I love, ___ take me all the way.
</pre>

Bridge

<pre>
A* Am G6 Fmaj7   A* Am   G6 Fmaj7
   Yeah. Yeah, ___ yeah. Oh, no, no, no, yeah, yeah.

A* Am   G6 Fmaj7 F5   E5   G5
Love me, I say, yeah, yeah.   One time.
</pre>

Chorus

<pre>
A**   Am7   G6*   Fmaj7*
(Under the bridge downtown,)   is where I drew some blood.

A**   Am7   G6*   Fmaj7*
(Under the bridge downtown,)   I could not get enough.

A**   Am7   G6*   Fmaj7*
(Under the bridge downtown,)   forgot about my love.

A**   Am7
(Under the bridge downtown,)

G6*   Fmaj7*   A** Am7 G6* Fmaj7*
  I gave my life away, ___ yeah, yeah, yeah.

A** Am7   G6* Fmaj7* A** Am7   G6* Fmaj7*
Oh, no, no, no, no, yeah, yeah.   Way down I said, oh, yeah, yeah.

A** Am7   G6* Fmaj7*
     Will I stay?
</pre>

Outro

<pre>
‖: A*   Am7 │ G6   Fmaj7 :‖ Play 4 times
│ A**
</pre>

Universally Speaking

Words and Music by Anthony Kiedis,
Flea, John Frusciante and Chad Smith

Melody:

saw your face, ___

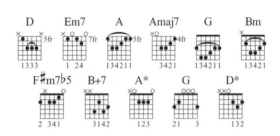

D   Em7   A   Amaj7   G   Bm

F#m7b5   B+7   A*   G   D*

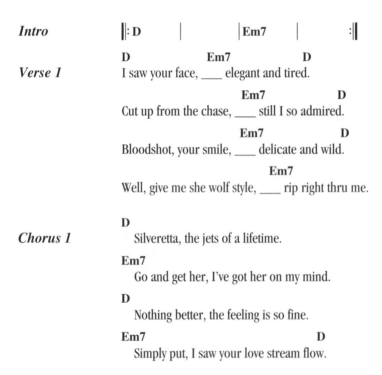

Intro   ‖: D | |Em7 | :‖

Verse 1
> D   Em7   D
> I saw your face, ___ elegant and tired.
>
>   Em7   D
> Cut up from the chase, ___ still I so admired.
>
>   Em7   D
> Bloodshot, your smile, ___ delicate and wild.
>
>   Em7
> Well, give me she wolf style, ___ rip right thru me.

Chorus 1
> D
>   Silveretta, the jets of a lifetime.
>
> Em7
>   Go and get her, I've got her on my mind.
>
> D
>   Nothing better, the feeling is so fine.
>
> Em7   D
>   Simply put, I saw your love stream flow.

© 2002 MOEBETOBLAME MUSIC
All Rights Reserved   Used by Permission

Bridge 1

A
Come on, baby, 'cause there's no name for…

Amaj7
Give it up and I got what I came for.

G   Bm
Universally speaking, ah.

A
Take it back and you make me nervous.

Amaj7
Nothing better than love and service.

G   Bm   F#m7♭5   B+7   Em
Universally speaking, I ____   win in the long run.

Interlude   *Repeat Intro*

Verse 2

D   Em7   D
I saw your crime, ____ dying to get high.

                Em7
Two of a kind ____ beats all hands tonight.

Chorus 2

D
Silveretta, the jets of a lifetime.

Em7
Go and get her, I've got her on my mind.

D
All the better to make it so fine.

Em7   D
Simply put, I saw your love stream flow.

Bridge 2   *Repeat Bridge 1*

Chorus 3

D
Silveretta, the jets of a lifetime.

Em7
Go and get her, I've got her on my mind.

D
Nothing better, the feeling is so fine.

Em7   D
Simply put, I saw your love stream flow.

Em7   D
Simply put, I saw your love stream flow. ____ Let's go.

Outro   ‖: A* | G | | D*   :‖ *Play 3 times*
                  | A* | G | | D*

Warped

Words and Music by Anthony Kiedis,
Flea, Chad Smith and David Navarro

Melody:

My tend - en - cy ___ for de-pend - en - cy

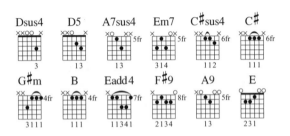

Dsus4   D5   A7sus4   Em7   C#sus4   C#

G#m   B   Eadd4   F#9   A9   E

Intro 1

| N.C.(E) | | | (Eadd9) | |
| (D) | (A) | |

Preamble

N.C.(E)   (G)   (E)
My tendency for dependency is offending me. It's upending me.

(G5)   (E)   (G5)
I'm pretending, see, to be strong and free ___ from my de-pendency.

It's warping me.

Intro 2

| N.C.(E7) | | | |
        Ho!

Verse 1

N.C.(E7)
So much love, so rare to dare, afraid of ever being there.

Take me home, I need repair. Take me, please, to anywhere.

Chorus 1

Dsus4 D5 Dsus4   D5 Dsus4   D5 Dsus4
        Descend _____ all the way,

D5 Dsus4 N.C.(E7)
All the way.   Woh!

© 1995 THREE POUNDS OF LOVE MUSIC
All Rights Reserved   Used by Permission

Verse 2

N.C.(E7)
Descended from demented men, struggle with the art of Zen.

Please don't look too close at me, you might not like what you see.

Chorus 2

Dsus4 D5 Dsus4   D5 Dsus4   D5 Dsus4 D5 Dsus4
     She said, _____ "All the way, all the way."

    D5 Dsus4 D5 Dsus4   D5 Dsus4 D5 Dsus4
Ev'- ry - day,   warped and scared

     D5 Dsus4 D5 Dsus4   D5 Dsus4   Dsus4 D5 Dsus4
Of be-ing there, _____ of be - ing there.

Guitar Solo ‖:N.C.(A5) | | | :‖ *Play 4 times*

|D5 |N.C.(E7)   A7sus4|N.C.(E7)   A7sus4|

|N.C.(E7) A7sus4 |N.C.(E7) A7sus4 |

Verse 3

N.C.(E7)
Craving sends me crawling, oh. Beg for mercy, does it show?

A vacancy that's full of holes. Hold me, please, I'm feeling cold.

Chorus 3

Dsus4 D5 Dsus4   D5 Dsus4   D5 Dsus4 D5 Dsus4
     She said, _____ "All the way, all the way."

    D5 Dsus4 D5 Dsus4   D5 Dsus4 D5 Dsus4
Ev'- ry - day,   warped and scared

     D5 Dsus4 D5 Dsus4   D5 Dsus4   D5 Dsus4 Em7
Of be-ing there, _____ of be - ing there.

Outro ‖:C#sus4 C# G#m | B   G#m   :‖

|Eadd4 | |F#9 | |

|A9 | |E |Em7

What It Is

Words and Music by
Anthony Kiedis and Flea

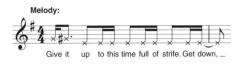

Melody:

Give it   up   to this time full of strife. Get down, _

E7#9   F#m

6fr

2 1 3 4   1 3 4 1 1 1

Verse 1

        E7#9
Give it up to this time full of strife.

Get down, you might be fucked up with the song of life.

Extend your deeper senses, there will be no fight

At the never ending ocean of perfect in-sights.

Round your mortal beam with a halo of light,

Till your animated aura will give delight.

Soon, your ev'ry single worry will be out of sight.

© 1982 MOEBETOBLAME MUSIC
All Rights Reserved   Used by Permission

Verse 2

E7#9

With the power of it we are about to astound,

All your preconceptions, they will come unbound.

"Listen very close," my inner voice expounds,

"We are the human race, and we groove to the sound."

Yes, we deliver the truth to my musical birth,

Our soul shocking sound will electrify the earth.

People have to know that it's not about money,

Cash is not the way to make your life sunny.

There is no need if you got the soul seed.

Love, life and peace, it can only begin

When you know in your heart that the change is within.

Love all your brothers and love all your sisters,

Love all the misses, and love all the misses.

And don't be shy when you're sharing your kisses,

Greed, jealousy gets boos and hisses.

Chorus 1

F#m
What it is, what it is, so much to be found.

What it is, what it is, groove down to the sounds.

What it is, what it is, what it is in a song.

                                              E7#9
What it is, what it is, you can do no wrong.

Verse 3

E7#9
Balance your life with the right kind of foods

To eat sad cow is to eat another you.

Well, that's an unfair rap, it's an unforgivable rude,

It'll put you karma in the worst of moods.

Someone drinking booze and taking too many ludes

'Cause when you cop , don't you cop an attitude,

And that's an ugly thing, it's not the real you.

So please, y'all, take some sound advice:

Be yourself, clear your mind, make a sacrifice,

                                          F#m
The always sober you is especially nice.

	E7#9
Verse 4	*Don't loot, don't shoot, give comet the boot,*

Verse 4　　　E7#9
Don't loot, don't shoot, give comet the boot,

I'd rather kickin' back between my bamboo flute.

Refuse to fight wars for political whores,

Unsurpassed peace lines the salt water shores.

It is my notion that the perfect peace potion

Can be found in the wake of the green tae motion.

Long rocky swells of the mighty blue ocean,

It's the cradle of peace, it's the perfect peace potion.

There you will find it, with sweet sea creatures,

The smile of a dolphin is a built in feature.

We will learn much peace with the whale as your teacher,

"Good mornin' class, how very nice to meet you."

Chorus 2　　　Repeat Chorus 1

Verse 5

E7#9
Open up your hearts to the planets, to the stars,

With your spirit take a trip from Venus to Mars.

You know, Einstein did while Hitler hid.

Now Albert lives forever in ev'ry single kid.

But with Adolph Hitler we are permanently rid.

Picasso, Mister Dali, and my man, Jimmy Hendrix,

These cool brothers make the world go 'round.

Yeah, they do it with art, and Jimmy did it with sound,

But by all these men it was found

Each and evr'y person can be just as renowned.

Don't let the world's racist creeds give your pretty face a frown.

Stand up to equal rights, I mean buckle down,

Go spread the word from town to town.

We are the human race and we groove to the sounds.

Outro

E7#9
Now that you've heard what it is in a song

From here on end you can do no wrong.

The Zephyr Song

Words and Music by
Anthony Kiedis, Flea,
John Frusciante and
Chad Smith

Melody:

Can I get your hand to write on, ___ just a piece of leg to bite on?

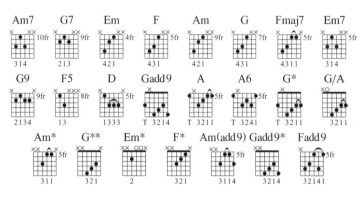

Intro

| Am7 | G7 | Em | F | |
| Am | G | Em | Fmaj7 | |

Verse 1

    Am7   G7
Can I get your hand to write on, ___ just a piece of leg to bite on?

    Em7   Fmaj7
What a night to fly my kite on. Do you want to flash a light on?

    Am7   G9
Take a look, it's on display ___ for you.

    Em7   F5
Comin' down, no not today.

    Am7   G7
Did you meet your fortune teller, ___ get it off with no propeller?

    Em7   Fmaj7
Do it up, it's on with Stella. What a way to finally smell her.

    Am7   G9
Pickin' up, but not too strong ___ for you.

    Em7   Fmaj7
Take a piece and pass it on.

© 2002 MOEBETOBLAME MUSIC
All Rights Reserved   Used by Permission

Chorus 1

D   Gadd9   A
Fly away on my zephyr,   I feel it more __ than ever.

D   Gadd9   A
And in this perfect weather,   we'll find a place __ together.

Interlude

Am7 G7 Em7 Fmaj7
Fly   on   my   wind.

Verse 2

Am7   G7
Rebel and a liberator, ___ find a way to be a skater.

Em7   Fmaj7
Rev it up to levitate her, superfriendly aviator.

Am7   G9
Take a look, it's on display ___ for you.

Em7   Fmaj7
Comin' down, no not today.

Chorus 2

D   Gadd9   A
Fly away on my zephyr,   I feel it more __ than ever.

D   Gadd9   A6
And in this perfect weather,   we'll find a place ___ together.

D
In the water where I center my emotion,

G*   A   G/A A
All the world can pass ___ me by.

D   G   Gadd9   A
Fly away on my zephyr,   we'll find ___ a place __ together.